BRIGHT IDEAS

Imaginative Writing

Written by Wes Magee

Published by Scholastic Ltd,
Villiers House, Clarendon Avenue,
Leamington Spa, Warwickshire CV32 5PR

© 1994 Scholastic Ltd
34567890 67890

Written by Wes Magee
Edited by Christine Lee
Sub-edited by Kate Banham
Illustrated by Mary Lonsdale
Designed by Micky Pledge
Front and back covers designed by
Sue Limb
Photograph by Martyn Chillmaid
Children's work provided by
Melanie Burgess, Louise Crampton,
Simon Crampton, Helena Lathbury,
Liz Walters and Rhiânnon Nicol
Artwork by Steve Williams Design, Leicester
Typeset by Typesetters (Birmingham) Ltd
Printed in Great Britain by Clays Ltd, St Ives plc

British Library Cataloguing in Publication Data
A catalogue record for this book is available from the
British Library.

ISBN 0-590-53079-8

The right of Wes Magee to be identified as
the Author of this work has been asserted
by him in accordance with the Copyright,
Designs and Patents Act 1988.

Contents

LOOKING, LISTENING AND TALKING 82

LETTERS AND MESSAGES 98

AN AUDIENCE FOR CHILDREN'S WRITING 108

REPRODUCIBLE MATERIAL AND RESOURCES 110

Introduction

During the 1960s and 1970s the widespread practice of 'creative writing' in schools drew criticism because it concentrated on free self-expression at the expense of language rules and structures. Since then changed attitudes and the National Curriculum have ensured a return to more level-headed educational thinking. It is now commonly agreed that children need to have a proper understanding of language in order to produce written work of quality.

The ideas for writing contained in this book seek to build on children's linguistic abilities by encouraging the use of the imagination. This can lead to the creation of interesting, language-enriched and even original work on the page.

No one expects children to attempt each and every idea outlined in this book, but sensible use of the suggestions throughout the year will add great variety to their written output. The many different ways of approaching stories, poems, lists and descriptions will help to keep the experience of writing alive and fresh. My main aim is not to train young writers to be poets and novelists, but rather to enlarge and enrich their use of language as an essential aid for day-to-day living.

CHILDREN WRITING

Writing isn't easy. It is a highly sophisticated form of communication between human beings. From their early years children are taught to understand the series of marks and squiggles we call writing. The great majority cope successfully with this intellectual activity, and from slow, laborious beginnings they progress to a point at which they can accomplish a wide range of written forms – stories, poems, informational writing, letters, lists, descriptions and reports.

Apart from the importance of being able to communicate with fellow human beings, imaginative writing offers children other benefits. It hones their powers of observation, gives training in thinking originally, and stretches and expands the imagination. Such writing also encourages self-examination and self-exploration in a complex world. Finally, imaginative writing develops a personal love of language and helps young readers to gain a deeper satisfaction from books.

STARTING POINTS FOR CHILDREN'S WRITING

Virtually anything can be used to spark off children's writing provided the teacher's input is sufficiently stimulating. Three principal starting points dominate the examples outlined int his book. They are:
● the physical world as perceived through a child's senses;
● a child's feelings and emotions
● a structure.

More specifically, starting points can be related to things experienced by and known to children. Such starters can include the following:
● the weather (e.g. a fall of snow);
● places (e.g. a woodland or a pond);
● calendar events (e.g. Pancake Day);
● pictures and sounds;
● natural objects (e.g. a fossil or a nest);
● people (e.g. a best friend);
● creatures (e.g. a snail or a blue whale);
● the emotions (e.g. feeling sad).

THE VARIETIES OF IMAGINATIVE WRITING

Even today, in some schools, children exist on a writing diet of 'the daily diary' and 'story'. Such restriction is unnecessary when other writing forms are so numerous and varied. Of course, story writing will always occupy a prime position, but children should have the chance to try their hands at composing lists, songs and chants, messages, dialogues, descriptions and poems. Poems alone can be endlessly varied – acrostics, haiku, couplets, through-the-week verses and image lists.

It is a great loss if teachers, busy as they are with a multitude of school activities, omit to present children with the chance to vary the form of their imaginative writings. The suggestions contained in this book are a ready-made resource for the teacher wishing to offer children fresh and challenging writing experiences.

Creating a writing atmosphere

Whatever the classroom situation – walled 'box', open plan, shared area – certain factors are important when children are trying to write imaginatively. They need space, time, the proper equipment and a stimulating input. Noise level is another key factor.

A beneficial and educative writing atmosphere comes about when the above-mentioned factors have been sorted out and distractions eliminated. Let us take a closer look at each factor.

Time to write

In an overloaded curriculum covering everything from the Pharaohs to PE, it is all too easy for writing sessions to become squeezed or rushed. The ghost story or poem acrostic just cannot be properly composed in a 15-minute 'window' before playtime. The teacher needs to set aside sufficient writing time to ensure the task's potential is fully realised. Young writers should be able to take note of any input, and then have time to respond, to think and to write.

Space to write

Cramped, untidy conditions will undoubtedly be reflected in a child's writing. Children need a proper amount of 'personal space', and that means a chair, table surface and room for personal equipment, such as paper, pens and pencils. If redrafting is to take place, then extra notebooks and sheets of paper increase the 'personal space' requirement. A sense of order and tidiness simply means that the young writer can concentrate fully on the writing task in hand.

The proper equipment

Nothing disrupts a writing atmosphere more than a desperate scramble or search for paper and pencils once the session has commenced. The teacher should

see that all writing requirements are readily available. This is all part of the organisational discipline from which children learn about 'doing a job properly'. Such writing equipment may well include rulers, pencils, pens, felt-tipped pens, note paper, word books, dictionaries and thesauruses.

Some types of writing (for example descriptions of a pebble or a stone) may require specialist equipment like magnifying lenses or pots of water. There may be a need for reference books. Again, availability of equipment requires forward planning.

The input

'Write a poem about the rain while I mark these maths books' is an instruction often heard in classrooms. Unfortunately, it is the kiss of death as far as imaginative writing is concerned.

The teacher should act as 'writing leader' and catch children's interest. This can often be achieved by talking or showing. The aim is to grab the children's attention in such a manner that they will want to listen and discuss, and then write. The initial enthusiasm and mental energy aroused by the teacher's input is crucial.

Noise level

Increased informality in schools and an altogether more user-friendly atmosphere have generally resulted in higher noise levels in the classroom. Children talk more readily. There is more movement about the classroom and around the building. Noise, however, distracts young writers. There is a need for a settled, quiet time to aid reflection and composition.

Writing is largely an individual activity, and while one must expect a tolerable 'working noise' level, it is essential to intervene when noise becomes unacceptable. External noise, such as banging doors or raised voices in the corridor, can destroy the 'writing atmosphere' by distracting the children's attention.

Teacher as role model

I have already mentioned the teacher's crucial role in generating interest, arousing enthusiasm and in creating a writing atmosphere. Once the children are busy writing there could well be an opportunity for the teacher to do likewise. Try your hand at some of the activities in this book, such as the matchbox list, the mini saga or the millions poem structure. You will quickly discover the problems that the children face. Moreover, a sense of togetherness or solidarity with the group or class will be experienced. Imaginative writing should be something the teacher attempts alongside the pupils; a oneness exists within the classroom.

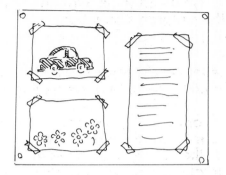

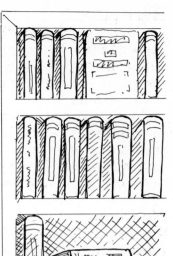
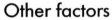

Other factors

There are a number of other factors which help to create the right atmosphere for writing.

● Books, attractively displayed and readily available, add greatly to the richness and atmosphere within a classroom. The variety of books – poetry, plays, short stories, novels, song lyrics, letters – show children the immense variety of published writing. Posters giving information about authors and their books are available from most publishers, and such visual material is usually attractive and bright.

● Displays of children's writing can act as examples and standard-setters. Is the handwriting in 'best'? Are the printed poems and stories well presented?

● The availability of one or more word processors helps to create the feel of a writer's study or office. Familiarity with the new technology means that young writers can present their work with varying typefaces. Such end-products look like professionally published pages and so enhance the writer's feeling of success and sense of achievement.

Problems in writing

Even in the best regulated classroom problems will arise where writing is concerned. They will mostly concern the following:
- lack of input;
- drying up;
- spelling;
- punctuation;
- drafting;
- distractions.

How should the teacher overcome such problems?

Lack of input

An interest-grabbing input by the teacher will fire the children's imaginations. Visual stimulation (such as a large coloured picture of a fox), a visit (for example to the school pond) or handling materials (such as a piece of tree bark) will enable the children to focus their thoughts. Lack of input means the young writers are left hungry. Simply, they haven't had enough 'school dinner for the mind'!

Drying up

That commonly-heard cry, 'I can't think what to write!' is avoided if the subject-matter (for example a ghost story) has been well discussed before writing commences. The input must be good, and a plan-of-action on the blackboard or sheet of paper (write about this, then this, and this, and this) helps to keep the pens hard at work. Most professional writers work to a plan, so why not young children?

Spelling

Keeping their own word books will give children a familiar spelling stand-by. Similarly, training in the use of a dictionary and a thesaurus gives young writers a large measure of independence. However, specific help for a particular subject, such as a story about dinosaurs, can be given by drawing up a 'word bank' list on the chalkboard or sheet of paper. The children themselves can suggest the words during the pre-writing discussion.

Punctuation

As with spelling, regular practice in the use of the punctuation code will give children the capability to structure their written work. Mistakes, of course, will be made, but with persistence and correction children can achieve mastery.

Drafting

I feel it is undesirable to redraft every piece of imaginative writing. Endless revising simply kills enthusiasm, quite apart from the fact that it is incredibly time-consuming. The sensitive teacher will know when to encourage note-making, drafting and redrafting, and when to require a once-only writing attempt.

Distractions

I have already mentioned how noise can distract young writers and so disturb the writing atmosphere. There are other distractions: other children working at different tasks within the same area or room; visitors entering the room; a sudden fall of snow in early December. In fact, the list of possible distractions is endless!

All the teacher can do is to work towards a writing atmosphere by controlling the factors as far as possible. It isn't always easy, but if the writing session gets underway and proceeds without too much interruption then the quality of the work produced is its own reward.

Starting with 'Me'

This opening chapter concentrates on the child's interest in him or herself. Children have a reservoir of knowledge about themselves, their experiences and their families. Without being over-intrusive it is a valuable learning activity to release such knowledge in the form of writing.

The chapter commences with the children themselves and moves on to give writing opportunities in connection with home life, the immediate family and wider relationships. There is a place for humour ('My wild week'), for predictions about the future ('Wannabes') and for physical observations ('My hand').

Face to face

Age range
Five to eleven.

Type of writing
Personal description.

What you need
Hand mirrors.

What to do
Let each child use a hand mirror to study his face. Allow for some initial hilarity, then ask the children to make brief notes about their hair (colour, length, style), eyes (colour, shape), eyebrows (length, shape), skin colouring and any marks or blemishes. Don't forget to examine noses, mouths, chins, ears and cheeks. Can the children see signs of bone structure?

Ask each child to refer to his notes and write a detailed description of his face. Suggest that a useful writing plan is to start at the top of the head and work downwards.

Follow-up
● Ask the children to add self-portraits to the descriptive writing. Once again let them use the hand mirrors to ensure the observational drawings are as accurate as possible.
● Make a 'Face to Face' class book. Include each piece of writing and self-portrait but omit all names. Number each page and add an index at the back of the book listing the names. The children can then try to identify each writer/artist before checking their suggestions against the index.
● Ask pairs of children to examine each other's face and write descriptions. Again, detailed observational sketches in pencil can be added.

The factfile

Age range
Six to eleven.

Type of writing
Completing a questionnaire.

What you need
Copies of photocopiable page 111.

What to do
Distribute copies of photocopiable page 111 and ask the children to complete the factfile. Their responses will range from one word to sentence length answers.

Follow-up
From the completed questionnaires extract the responses to one question and make a block graph to indicate the children's preferences.

Insults!

Age range
Six to eleven.

Type of writing
A poem structure.

What you need
No special equipment.

What to do
This activity offers an opportunity to use children's love of the insult. All too often they use insults destructively and cause upset and hurt. By using this traditional form of African insult in a writing structure the children can work within an acceptable convention.

Explain that each verse of their poem should begin with an exclamation 'You!', and that thereafter the writer should use the key word 'like' to create word pictures for facial features (Figure 1).

INSULTS !

You!

Your hair is like a tangly mop-head.

You!

Your eyes are like mini fried eggs.

Figure 1

Older children can be encouraged to try to extend the word pictures, thus building up a more detailed description while keeping the sense intact (Figure 2).

Tell the children that their insult writing can include all the facial features (mouth, teeth, eyes, cheeks, lips, brow, chin), or can extend to cover parts of the body (legs, arms, toes, feet, fingers, chest, shoulders, bottom).

Insults

You!
Your head is like a rotting
wooden barrel full of straggly
weeds on a garden patio.

You!
Your eyebrows are like
dried-out strips of seaweed
left lying on the beach
at high tide.

Figure 2

Follow-up
Let the children illustrate one or more of the verses.
'Your teeth are like tombstones', for example, offers
scope for imaginative drawings. Use of coloured pencils
or felt-tipped pens will enhance the end-product.

Family photograph

Age range
Six to eleven.

Type of writing
Imaginative prose.

What you need
A selection of family photographs.

What to do
Ask each child to try to bring a family photograph to
school. Some snaps will show an extended family
(children, parents, grandparents), or a nuclear family
unit or even the family pet.

Explain that whatever the composition of the
photographs, the idea is for the children to write about
something funny associated with each person (or just
one person or a pet) in the snap. Layout of the writing,
as always, gives young writers a framework around
which to organise their thoughts.

My Mum

Once she pulled on her trousers and they split right along the seam at her bottom. There was a terrible ripping noise. "I Must be getting fat," she said, and dropped the trousers into the bin!

My Cat, Thumbelina

Thumbelina loves climbing into cardboard boxes. When we bring home the shopping from 'Simpkins' and unpack, she jumps into the empty box. She sits there with just her black, pointed ears showing over the top!

The baby

In the photograph I am sitting in an old pram, in a back garden. I think I am about six months old. I am wearing a woollen hat, and I'm holding a round, plastic rattle in my little hand.

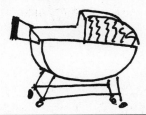

A variation would be to ask children to bring in photos of themselves as babies. Such snaps are always a source of great fascination, not least because the children can barely recognise themselves. It takes an imaginative leap to write about what it was like to be a baby. Pre-writing discussion in the classroom will enable the children to clarify their ideas. Writing that is half-descriptive and half-imaginative can then proceed.

Follow-up
Set up a wall display of 'baby' photos, adding a name beneath each snap. Some babies will probably be recognisable while others will look nothing like the named child! Examples of the children's written descriptions can be mounted alongside.

Books about babies and family life (often with wonderful illustrations) can be added to the display.

My wild week

Age range
Eight to eleven.

Type of writing
Creative diary entries.

What you need
Copies of photocopiable page 112.

What to do
Diary writing by children can be stunningly dull. 'Monday: Got up. Had toast for breakfast. Went to school. I was bored. Came home. Went to bed.' It reads rather like a quote from the headteacher's logbook! In some schools, children regularly write their 'daily diary'. While this ensures that writing takes place, such communication often tends to be basic and lacking in zest, life and energy.

In order to add some zip, get the children to attempt weird diary entries. Challenge them to write a diary for a 'wild week' using the format on photocopiable page 112. Explain that each entry can begin with something ordinary ('Got up . . .', or 'At school today . . .') but that following on from that, the diary entry should be entirely imaginary. Stress the fact that the more zany the entry the better.

My Wild Week

MONDAY: Got up and boarded an Intergalactic Airways flight to Saturn's 6th moon. We travelled by time-slip which meant we arrived in 7½ minutes. The moon, which is called Turtletopz, is green and made entirely of soft chilly stuff, a bit like ice-cream.

TUESDAY: At Brownies we played 'Eat-a-chair' and Emma Bigbaggs gobbled her wood and steel chair in four gulps. I managed to munch my way through the plastic seat quite quickly, but some metal nuts and bolts got caught in my throat.

Follow-up

• Ask the children to bring in diaries from home. A wide variety can be collected, and maybe even one with a lock and key. There will be pocket diaries, calendar note diaries, desk diaries, and so on. An interesting collection can be displayed on a table along with various calendars. If possible, borrow the school's logbook to include with the display.

• Extra learning opportunities can be made by listing special days in the year (for example Pancake Day, Easter Monday, Hallowe'en).

• Make a list of the children's birthdays to help reinforce the months of the year. Add a similar list showing the birthdates of famous people.

Grans and Grandads

Age range
Five to eleven.

Type of writing
Character description.

What you need
No special equipment.

What to do
Even in times when the extended family appears to be threatened with extinction, children generally retain a very soft spot for grandparents. Parents are all too often caught up in the rush and bustle of day-to-day living, and grandparents seem to offer children a haven of attention and kindness. Affection between children and their grandparents remains strong.

Ask the children to write about a gran or a grandad and explain that the character description should communicate the person's habits, idiosyncrasies and activities. Encourage discussion before they begin to write. Help the children to structure their work by writing up on the board a 'staircase' of questions as follows;

What is gran's (or grandad's) name?
Where does she live?
What is her house (or flat) like?
What does she look like?
What is her hair like?
What does she wear?
What does she like to eat and drink?
Does she have any little sayings?
Has she any prized possessions?
Does she do anything funny?
Why do you like her?

Using the 'stairs' the child's writing may well commence thus:

My Gran
My gran is called Gran Moffat and she lives at number 12, Railway Cuttings in . . .

Follow-up
Make a collection of the things the children's grans and grandads say. Over a period of time the children will remember and contribute remarks such as 'Well, I never did!', and 'We've seen the best of this old world'. Keep a 'running list' so that the children can add new remarks as they are gathered.

Fibs, lies and porky pies

Age range
Seven to eleven.

Type of writing
A poem structure.

What you need
No special equipment.

What to do
Telling lies, fibs or porkies is one of those human traits which can be nasty or nice. Lies, on one hand, can be devious; on the other hand they can exaggerate for effect.

'I didn't steal her money,' if untrue, is nasty. Whereas 'I ran to school faster than the wind,' is an acceptably colourful statement of non-fact.

Make use of the children's ability to fib by setting them the task of telling porkies about someone they know well. The person could be a family member, a friend, the teacher, the school cleaner or even the headteacher. Explain that the idea is to 'see' the chosen person in unusual terms, for example, as a fruit, or as a place to go on holiday. From the children's suggestions draw up a list of 'subject areas'. This might include any of the following:
● a drink;
● a type of weather;
● a kind of animal;
● a type of food;
● a piece of furniture;
● a sound or a noise;
● a bird;
● a fruit;
● a place to go on holiday.
Ask the children to write a poem based around these subject areas, developing the 'porky' in each instance, and at the same time creating a poem shape. A completed piece of work may appear as follows:

My friend, Annabel
She is a kitchen chair,
   made of pine, square-shaped,
     with a fluffy pink cushion
      and a shiny polish.

    My friend, Annabel,
   is a sleek magpie,
brightly feathered, very shy,
and gliding smoothly through the day.

My friend is a plate of salad,
   cool and crisp lettuce . . .

Wannabes

Age range
Six to eleven.

Type of writing
Descriptive prose.

What you need
No special equipment.

What to do
Even in times of high unemployment, children still want to be something when they grow up. Hope springs eternal, and 'wannabes' are thick on the ground.

Ask the children what they would like to be. Doubtless their preferences will weigh heavily in favour of models, pop stars, footballers, policemen, soap actors, astronauts, mums and even Prime Ministers. I can't see too many opting for estate agents or traffic wardens — television personalities are more likely role models.

Explain that the shape and verse pattern should continue down the page. The poem involves both the use of imagination, and a specific structure of four lines per verse to follow. Can the child begin each verse in a different way ('She is . . .', 'Annabel . . .')? Explain that such variations help to keep the writing fresh and lively.

Follow-up
Ask the children to make a painting of the person in their poems. Thus, Annabel can be depicted as a plate of salad, with her name printed beneath!

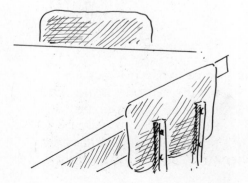

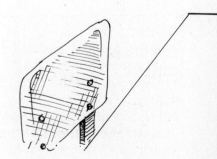

Invite the children to write about their 'I wannabe . . .' wishes. Suggest using the four 'Ws' to maintain the writing flow:
- Who?
- Why?
- Where?
- When?

Follow-up
Draw up a class list of 'I wannabe . . .' preferences, then let the children add coloured drawings of themselves as their chosen 'wannabe'.

Like . . . and don't like

Age range
Six to eleven.

Type of writing
Comparisons list.

What you need
No special equipment.

What to do
Children may not have definite opinions about the ERM or VAT but they do know what they like and dislike. *Neighbours* is a like, while *Panorama* is a dislike. Opinions will be clear cut.

Ask children to list their likes and dislikes, and follow each item with the word 'because' (Figure 1). Thus they are required to give a reason, or reasons. The process goes beyond mere choice and ensures the written responses are not just single words.

I like . . . and don't like
I like cartoons on TV because . . .

....

I don't like prunes because.....................................

....

I like choc ices because...

....

I don't like cabbage because ....

....

Figure 1

Such comparisons lists can become lengthy when the children have free choice for their writing. In order to focus attention try setting various subjects, such as the night, trees, smoke, cup of tea, ice skating, a leopard, the zoo, a pair of socks. Ask the writers to think hard and come up with reasons for liking *and* disliking the same thing. Once again, a writing pattern on the page helps the children to organise their thoughts (Figure 2).

I like . . . and don't like
I like having a bath because.....................................

....
  I don't like having a bath because.............................

  ....
I like trees because ....

....
  I don't like trees because...

  ....

Figure 2

Follow-up
Let the children form two groups on either side of the classroom (or school hall in a morning assembly), then ask them to take turns to read out their likes and dislikes.

My hand

Age range
Six to nine.

Type of writing
A long list.

What you need
Adhesive or word processor that prints on to a continuous sheet.

What to do
Ask the children to try to view their hands as independent life forms. What does the hand do? Where does it go? What does it touch and feel? Can it be nasty, nice, sad or excited? What work does it do? Has it got bad habits? Where does it hide? Classroom discussion will quickly draw forth dozens of answers.

Then ask the children to write an on-going list. Such a listing is virtually inexhaustible. Once the children start writing, they will find this task easy and should be able to complete a full page, or two, three, four or more pages. If the pages are loose they can be stuck together to make a long, roll-up scroll. On the word processor they can be printed off on to a similarly long sheet. When held at full stretch the list can be taller than the writer!

My hand

My hand turns a key in the
lock,

it peels a satsuma,

it waves goodbye to my
friends,

it can make a fist and
punch something,

it scratches my head,

it picks my nose,

it points the way to the
shops,

it turns the page of a
book.

Follow-up

● Add a closely-observed drawing of the writer's hand. Trace around the hand in order to make a life-size shape and then add lines, marks and wrinkles. The children's hand shapes can be cut out and mounted to form a 'massed hands' picture. The long lists can be suspended from the ceiling or draped down the walls.
● Collect pictures from newspapers and magazines in which people are seen using their hands (pointing, waving, applauding, threatening, indicating). A word list beside the collection will help to extend the children's vocabulary.

My teacher

Age range
Six to eleven.

Type of writing
Description.

What you need
No special equipment.

What to do
If you feel able to take the strain, allow the children to write a description of you or another member of staff. Such descriptions need not be lengthy – a single page should suffice. Offer the children a few ideas, such as the following:
- a physical description;
- clothing;
- the way you speak, including any habitual sayings (e.g., 'Okay, zoo members!');
- mannerisms and habits (e.g., index finger used as a pointer; tugging the left ear);
- anything odd, funny or peculiar.

Such writing indicates a level of trust between child and teacher, so explain that it should not be rude or offensive! (In fact, whenever I have set up such a writing session I have invariably found the youngsters expressing their liking, affection and support for the teacher.)

If other people (such as headteacher, school cook, crossing patrol person or caretaker) are used as writing subjects, a series of 'identikits' can be completed.

Follow-up
Let the children paint or draw the teacher. Display the art work alongside the written descriptions for all to enjoy. Because of the 'personal' nature of the work it is always popular as reading matter with other members of the class.

Display a collection of books, both stories and poems, which take teachers and school life as their subject. There are many, many books in this category.

When I'm 99¾ years old . . .

Age range
Seven to eleven.

Type of writing
Imaginative description and list.

What you need
No special equipment.

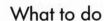

What to do
Old age, to children, seems a lifetime away. It is! Can they imagine what it is like to be really old? Pre-writing discussion will enable children to talk about old people they know.

After the discussion, ask the children to write about what they would do if they were 99¾ years old. They could do what they've always wanted to do. The writing can be part description, part list and the children should group their ideas in threes. For instance:

When I'm 99¾ years old . . .
  I will
eat 21 slices of fried Danish bacon,
wear size 17 sky-blue-with-red-spots wellies,
sleep out all night in a tree house.
  I will
leave my bedroom light on all day,
kiss the lollipop man on the zebra crossing,
never ever cut the front lawn grass.

Follow-up
● Invite a couple of elderly people into school to talk to the children about their lives. These guests could be people known to you or elderly relatives of one of the children. Ask the children to prepare some questions to ask their guests.

Some of the youngsters can then read out their written work. Can the old people say what they would most like to do?
● If the school has a Polaroid camera the children can take photographs of the elderly guests talking to other members of the class. These snapshots can be displayed alongside the children's completed writings.

Stories

Story goes back to the earliest of times; human beings have always been attracted to tales, legends, fables and myths. Children, in their own way, can add to this human continuum by writing stories based on a series of 'starter' ideas.

Many contemporary story writers experiment with the story form and, in doing so, attempt to alter well-worn structures. Where children are concerned it is best to keep things simple and straightforward. Thus, a story should have a beginning, a middle and an ending.

The suggestions in this chapter vary from a story form giving directions ('The way to the haunted house'), through list stories ('The materials monster'), to the purely imaginative ('In Winterland').

The way to the haunted house

Age range
Seven to eleven.

Type of writing
A journey, with directions.

What you need
Copies of photocopiable
page 113.

What to do
Explain to the children that for once they are going to
forget the ghost which inhabits the haunted house, and
concentrate instead on giving directions for reaching the
establishment. Ask them to begin by making notes about
the following points.

● Where does the journey start? Invent a place (for
example, Scaretown or Shiversville).
● What kind of path leads to the haunted house
(muddy lane, brambly path)?
● List and name all the places passed on the journey.
Include a woodland (for example, The Hanging Man's
Wood), a lake or pond, a rocky crag, a cliff, a marsh,
swamp or bog or a ruined building.
● List all the creatures encountered on the journey (owl,
fox, badger, spiders). Give each creature a weird
characteristic and a colour (such as, an indigo owl with
an eye patch).

The Way to the Haunted House

Start your journey at the tiny post office in the village of Fright. Follow the crooked and broken signpot pointing to Hanging Man's Wood. The path leading to the wood is riddled with potholes and puddles. Briars and brambles will rip your clothes if your not careful. The path is terribly twisty. The wood is gloomy and eerily quiet.

Boo!

Figure 1

Encourage the children to refer to their notes as they write the story and compose imaginative descriptions. Each place to be passed can perhaps signal the start of a new paragraph. Explain that the aim of the story is to show how a 'reader' could successfully and safely reach the haunted house. Stress that the writer must indicate the various dangers along the way (the sinking, sucking mud of the foul swamp with the octopus odours). Arrival at the haunted house brings the story writing to a close.

The journey could well commence as in Figure 1.

Follow-up

Give each child a copy of the map on photocopiable page 113. Ask them to devise names for the features marked and to draw on the route they might take to the haunted house. They can also add mini-pictures of the creatures they meet along the way.

In Winterland

Age range
Nine to eleven.

Type of writing
Adventure story.

What you need
Ice cubes, a plate.

What to do
Show the children a pile of ice cubes on a plate and let them each have an opportunity to touch and feel the ice. Explain that the ice comes from a magical country called Winterland. Ask them to think what Winterland might be like by asking questions such as the following:
● Where is Winterland (e.g., beyond snow-covered mountains)?
● How does one enter Winterland (e.g., through a snowy doorway set in a snowman's tummy)?
● Who lives there (e.g., small, bluish ice people with icicle fingers)?
● What's the weather like (e.g., freezing cold, no sunshine, green sky)?
● What dangers threaten the Winterlanders (e.g., the Hotspotters who dwell in a distant volcano)?
● Does a battle take place? Where (e.g., on a permanently frozen lake)?
● What's the outcome? How is Winterland saved?
   Ask the children to use their answers and suggestions to help them write stories about Winterland. Explain that use of paragraphs based on the questions will give the narrative 'breathing spaces' on the page.

> It snowed all night and the next day. When it stopped I built a massive snowman; 'Frozentoes'! I threw snowballs at him. I hit his snowy face but when I hit his snowy tummy a doorway flew open scattering fluffs of snow.

Figure 1

   Personal involvement is added if the children themselves are characters in the story. The adventure could begin as in Figure 1.

Follow-up

Help the children to make a three-dimensional picture or diorama of a scene from Winterland by first drawing, and then colouring, a background showing the green sky, snow-covered mountains and ice people on the frozen lake. Then stick empty matchboxes (or wads of paper) to each corner. On these mount a 'window' sheet of polythene. You can then look into Winterland.

A mini saga

Age range
Seven to eleven.

Type of writing
A short story in exactly 50 words.

What you need
No special equipment.

What to do
Some years ago the BBC launched a 'mini saga' writing competition in which entrants had to use exactly 50 words. Some memorable pieces of writing resulted. The mini saga is the very opposite of the long, leisurely narrative. It demands economy of word usage and precise communication.

Give the young writers a choice of subjects such as the following:
- A landing on planet Mars;
- The evening the television exploded;
- The invasion of the Rat Nose Smogs from Jupiter;
- The school disco;
- The creature in the garden pond.

Tell the children to include the following ingredients in their mini sagas:
- a place or location (the setting);
- a time of day or night, or a particular day;
- the character or characters;
- what happened (the events).

Explain that because of the concise nature of the work, it is best to draft the story using *more* than 50 words. It can then be revised (and rewritten, if necessary) until the word count is exactly 50. Let the children add an illustration or even a series of mini pictures (like a comic strip) to the saga.

Follow-up
Encourage the children to search for short stories in books in the classroom or library. What is the shortest published story they can find? How many words has the writer used?

The beast in the boiler house

Age range
Seven to eleven.

Type of writing
Spooky story.

What you need
An organised visit to the school's boiler house.

What to do
Most schools have a resident scare thing, or so it is rumoured. The 'beast in the boiler house' is a common enough fantasy which has seeped its way into a number of published stories and poems. If your school doesn't have a boiler house then use a substitute. For example:
● The spook in the shed;
● The haunter in the headteacher's room;
● The ogre in the office;
● The bogey in the bike shed;
● The spectre in the staffroom;
● The hag in the hall.

Imaginations will be stirred considerably if a visit to the site (boiler house, staff room) can be arranged. Once the ingredients have been established then story writing can proceed.

Pre-writing discussion will help to establish the nature and extent of the story. Explain that it should be a scary story, but without bolts of blood and bevies of bodies. Encourage the young writers to be devious in their narratives, to avoid blatant gore but make use of atmosphere to create fear. For example, mysterious noises can be heard, strange things found or footprints discovered. The actual horror itself (be it beast, ogre or haunter) can even remain unseen until the very end.

The children will need to use certain ingredients in their narratives:
● a setting (where in the school?);
● the time (during school hours? at dawn?);
● the characters (the child? caretaker? cleaner? teacher? group of children?).

Again, the use of paragraphs will help the youngsters to plan their work.

Such story writing can be lengthy. It can be written over a period of a week, or even longer. This gives opportunities for a story making use of chapters, and for real development in the events and action.

Follow-up

If the stories look promising it could be worthwhile printing them out on the word processor. The narratives can then be cut and mounted on pages to make individual books. The text could be illustrated and a cover made bearing the title and the author's name. The back cover could include a sketch of the author (or an actual photograph), a brief 'blurb' résumé of the story, price, a made-up ISBN (International Standard Book Number) and the name of an invented publishing company.

Such books, containing well-written, crafted stories and illustrations become treasured art objects in their own right. Also, they do wonders for school/class/home relationships as they are an indication of quality work.

The longest story in the world

Age range
Five to eleven.

Type of writing
A collaborative class story.

What you need
Word processor, drawing materials.

What to do
Ask each child in the class, or groups of children, to write a section or a chapter of a story. Explain that the chapters need not be long, say a page each. The chapters can be either handwritten or word processor printed and then joined to make a long, single sheet which may very well stretch the length of the classroom.

The first task is to select a subject. If, for example, the chosen subject is '*The Adventures of the Tricky Twins on Planet Trickk*', pre-writing discussion will clearly establish the two principal characters. Who are they? Where are they from? How old are they? What do they wear? How did they reach Planet Trickk?

It could be useful for the children to draw the Tricky Twins *before* writing takes place, during a separate art session perhaps. With the characters visually established, the young writers can each imagine an adventure and write it up. In effect, each writer or group of writers will be creating their own short story. Common ground for the stories will be the setting (Planet Trickk) and the principal characters (the Tricky Twins).

Get the children to add drawings of the Tricky Twins to the long story sheet, including drawings for each adventure.

Follow-up

If possible, display the longest story in the world in the school hall or corridor where it can be admired by the rest of the school.

It could also make a great news item for the local newspaper. Usually a telephone call to the reporters' desk will produce a visit from a journalist and a photographer. In this way the longest story in the world can also be a good PR vehicle for the school.

A picture story-book

Age range
Seven to eleven.

Type of writing
A story for young children.

What you need
Drawing materials, a selection of picture books, card, scissors, photocopiable pages 114 and 115.

What to do
Let the children try their hands at writing and illustrating a legend or fairy tale for four- and five-year-olds. In order to concentrate on the level of simple communication required it is perhaps best to retell one of the well-known stories, such as 'Little Red Riding Hood' or 'The Three Little Pigs'. Show the children picture book versions of such stories, and then let them attempt a simple rewrite.

When the stories are finished, ask the children to divide them into 16 sections. Using photocopiable page 114, give each child four sheets of paper, printed front and back, and ask them to fold the sheets in half to make a 16 page book. Get them to number the pages and write up the story, one section to each page, then illustrate each page.

Give the children copies of photocopiable page 115 to make a front and back cover, then decorate them with the story title, the writers' and illustrators' names, price and the publisher. On the back cover ask them to add a made-up ISBN and bar code, a 'blurb' résumé of the story and a picture of the author. Inside the front cover add the date of publication, the © sign and the publisher's address.

Once the books are finished, let the children present them to younger children in the school (or at another school) for them to read and enjoy. Simple 'thank you' letters in return complete a most satisfying project all round.

Follow-up
Set up a display of picture story-books. In this way older children can enjoy again books they read some years ago and also observe all the details that go into book production and publication.

The materials monster

Age range
Seven to eleven.

Type of writing
A story with chapters.

What you need
A copy of *The Iron Man* by Ted Hughes.

What to do
Ted Hughes' famous story *The Iron Man* is known throughout the land and can be found in virtually every school. Read the opening few pages to the children to remind them of the Iron Man's construction.

Ask the children to invent their own larger-than-life constructed monsters made of lots of different materials. Ask the children to begin by listing appropriate materials. Suggest that they include things made of wood, iron, steel, rubber, cloth, glass, pottery, cardboard, plastic, leather, brass and copper.

Once the list is complete, let them proceed to write Part One of the story.

Part Two of the story should relate to what the Materials Monster does, while Part Three can tell how the Monster meets its end.

Writing a story in three parts in this way will help children to understand about chapter divisions. Of course, the story can be longer than three chapters if required. More able writers will be able to complete four, five and even six chapters, thus making a really substantial story.

> My materials Monster
> Part one. How it was made
> My Materials Monster's head is a plastic dustbin with a tangle of green garden twine and thick blue wool for hair. Her eyebrows are two bent steel forks. Her eyes are tarnished old-fashioned brass door knobs from a junk shop.

Follow-up
● Invite the children to bring materials to school and co-operate in the building of a Materials Monster. The monster will probably be quite tall and so will need to be propped up, while the various parts will need to be securely fastened together. Cardboard boxes can be used to make a basic Monster shape, then various materials and objects can be attached to it. Any left over materials (bicycle tyre, tin bucket, old mop, carpet squares, plastic containers and so on) can be piled up at the Monster's feet.
● Let the children record their stories on to cassette. The cassette player can be placed next to the monster display so that other children can play back the tape and listen to the stories.
● Collect stories and poems about monsters and display them. There will be dozens on the classroom bookshelves and in the school library.

The life of . . .

Age range
Nine to eleven.

Type of writing
Biographical story.

What you need
A children's novel, chalkboard or large sheet of paper.

What to do
Read to the children an extract from a novel in which one of the characters is revealed. It could, for instance, be an extract about James from Roald Dahl's *James and the Giant Peach*, about Szolda from David Line's *Run for your life* or about Roberta from E. Nesbit's *The Railway Children*. The reading should give the children a taste of the character and initiate a classroom discussion.

Next, pose certain questions on the board or on a large sheet of paper. The questions should be designed to get the children thinking, and then writing, about the character. If, for example, you read an extract detailing the character Blind Pew from Robert L. Stevenson's *Treasure Island*, you might ask the following questions.
- What does Blind Pew look like?
- Where does he live?
- What does he wear?
- What does he eat and drink?
- Who are his friends, or enemies?
- Does he own any animals or pets?
- What problems (illness?) or difficulties (money?) does he have to face?

Now ask the children to write stories about the character, using the questions as a plan around which their imaginations must work.

Such a character description (part biographical, part imaginative) can become lengthy as the young writers become involved with the life and times of the person.

Follow-up
- Ask the children to paint portraits of the character. Design, cut out and stick on a frame. As with real portraits in a stately home, get them to add a name plaque giving the name of the character, the name of the artist and the date beneath the frame.
- Gather and display books featuring the children's favourite characters. Such a collection may include many characters ranging from Tin Tin to the Borrowers and William.

The green ghost

Age range
Seven to eleven.

Type of writing
Ghost story.

What you need
No special equipment.

What to do
Suggest that the children write a story about a green ghost. Explain that this time there is no plan of action, no list of helpful notes. For once, the writers should ignore forward planning and just let their imaginations flow freely. Once the location and the characters are established, the storyline should develop swiftly.

Use the oddity of a 'green' ghost to give the story an extra twist. Ask the children why the ghost should be green. Explain that they must use their ingenuity to work it into the story.

The troll

Age range
Eight to eleven.

Type of writing
Legend.

What you need
Books of legends (or fables).

What to do
Read a fable or legend to the class. This may be a tale from the Brothers Grimm or one of Ulysses' adventures. Later on (the next day, perhaps) initiate a brief discussion about the legend. Ask the children to say what 'ingredients' they noticed in the story. They may well mention characters, a setting, a mysterious or magical element, danger, a weird being or creature, and the outcome or ending.

Now introduce the 'troll' as a character from legend. Trolls, as cuddly little toys, have become popular in recent years, and children are familiar with the strange beings from Scandinavian folklore. Here you could talk about the story of the 'Three Billy Goats Gruff' and their attempts to cross a bridge, beneath which skulked a hungry troll.

Now ask the children to create their own 'troll' legends. The following guidelines will give them a framework on which to base their stories.
- The troll lives under a bridge in Norway. Describe his home.
- The troll won't permit people to cross the bridge. Why not?
- Some people wish to cross the bridge. Who are they? Why do they want to cross?
- What happens? What does the troll do?
- How is the troll outwitted?

Such a legend can continue for two or three pages provided the children are really involved in the writing task. They may like to add illustrations. These can be a series of mini pictures depicting the various stages of the story.

Follow-up
Set up a display of books containing legends and fables. Include books of fairy stories (legends under another name). Over a period of a month the children can dip into this collection and read the published stories. Ask them to state which is their favourite legend. Which legend is the most popular?

The working children

Age range
Seven to eleven.

Type of writing
A historical story.

What you need
History books (about the Victorian age).

What to do
Let the children study the books on the Victorians. They will certainly encounter the 'working children' and their hard lives as chimney-sweeps and mine and mill workers. In small groups the children should then discuss and draw up an outline for a story set towards the end of the nineteenth century. They will need to decide the following:
- Where is the story set (in a mine? in a mill?)?
- Who are the characters? (Include a boy and a girl as the working children. Make them brother and sister. They are orphans.)
- What happens to the two children?
- Who treats them badly?
- Who shows them kindness?
- Include an animal in the story (cat? dog? goose?).
- What happens (the events)?
- How does the story end?

Once they have outlined the story it can be written up either individually or as a group. If undertaken as a group activity, the story can eventually be put on the word processor and copies printed out for each child. The children can then add their own illustrations to the text.

Follow-up
Hold a dressing-up competition. Ask parents for any old clothes they may wish to throw out. The children can cut these up to make ragged costumes and use them to dress up as Victorian waifs. Who manages to create the best effect?

Organise a 'working children' parade in the school hall. Set up a catwalk and let each child display his or her costume for the audience.

Poems and songs

Rhythm and rhyme have always been attractive to children. Even in this technological age, playgrounds still resound with chants, counting-out rounds, skipping rhymes and raps. Children can, at appropriate moments, write freely and expressively in the style of free verse poems, but I feel it is more commonly useful to give a verse structure around which to gather their thoughts, observations and imaginings.

The activities in this chapter range from shape writing ('Climb the mountain') to 'found' poems. Each idea offers the young writers stimulation from which they can proceed to develop original and exciting words on the page.

Playtime!

Age range
Six to eleven.

Type of writing
A list poem.

What you need
Chalkboard or large sheet of paper, word processor.

What to do
Ask the children to name the games they play at playtime. As an aid to writing it is useful to list the class's (or the group's) suggestions. Activities will probably include hopscotch, stuck-in-the-mud, football, skipping, it, catch, netball, chasing, and so on. Ask them to name other activities undertaken which might involve the emotions, or person-to-person confrontations, such as squabbling, crying, fighting, pushing, pinching, kissing, hugging, poking, shouting, squealing and moaning.

Explain that the children are going to write poems about playtime and that each line of the poem should begin with a child's name followed by a brief description of what the child is doing. Ask them to use no more than five words in each line. The poem will take shape as follows:

Keith is standing on his head.
Caroline shoots at netball.
Andy's nose is dripping blood.
Ranji swaps his marbles.

Alternatively, the poem could be undertaken as a class collaboration with each child contributing two lines. It could then be typed up on the word processor.

A more difficult task would be to make the poem rhyme. A four-line verse with a rhyme scheme ABCB is worth attempting as below.

Matthew kicks the football.
Li Chung gives a sneeze.
Debbie does the double-skip.
Shaun has grazed his knees.

Follow-up

● A group of children could draw and colour the playground background on a large sheet of paper. Then the whole of the class could be invited to draw themselves doing one of the actions mentioned in the poem. The drawings could then be cut out and mounted against the playground background.
● Make a list of present-day playground games and one of old-fashioned games (for example, whip-and-top, five stones, hula-hoops). Parents and grandparents are a source for such information.
● Write out and collect (in a book or on a wall-board) playground chants and rhymes currently in use. Some will be associated with skipping, while others are used in 'counting out' rituals.

Climb the mountain

Age range
Seven to eleven.

Type of writing
Shape poem.

What you need
Pictures of hills and mountains, chalkboard, copies of photocopiable page 116.

What to do
Show the children pictures of hills and mountains, and then draw from them words connected with such places, for example peak, summit, outcrop, scree, steep, rough, rugged, high. Write the words on the chalkboard.

Ask the children to use the words to help them write a simple description of mountain climbing, no more than four or five lines in length. (Because the description is short it can easily be revised and rewritten within a session.)

Next, give the children the photocopied sheets for them to present their writing in a mountain shape. Explain that the first word should be written in the bottom left-hand corner and that the description should gradually climb the mountain until the summit is reached. Thereafter the words should descend down the frame, as in Figure 1.

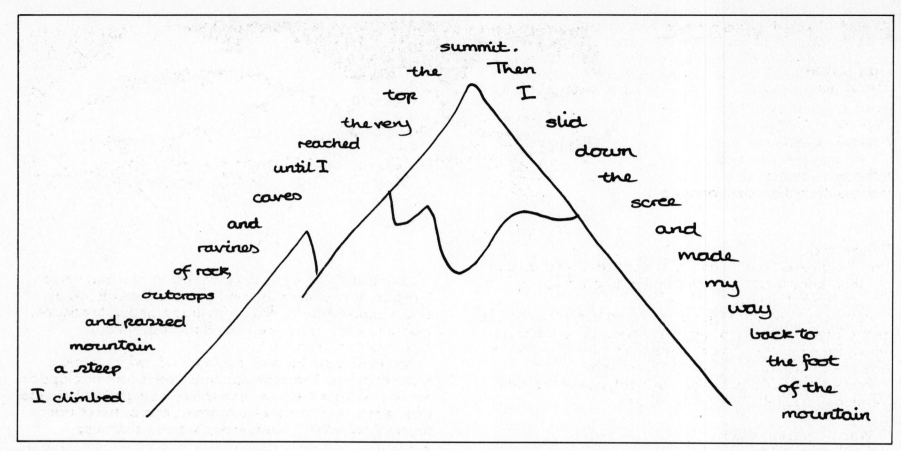

summit.

the Then

top I

the very slid

reached down

until I the

caves scree

and and

ravines made

of rock, my

outcrops way

and passed back to

mountain the foot

a steep of the

I climbed mountain

Figure 1

The children could then go on to write four-line rhyming poems and then plot them in the mountain shape. An example could well be as in Figure 2.

I climb the mountain high.
See the clouds, and touch the sky.
I feel the wind against me blow.
See the green fields far below.

Figure 2

Follow-up
● Let the children add illustrations to show people climbing the mountain of words.
● Mount the children's shape writing alongside drawings of mountain ranges. Shading can be used to indicate steepness and shadow. To the display add photographs of hills and mountains from magazines or books, pictures of famous mountaineers and items of equipment such as ropes, boots, haversack, tent.

Bad, bad weather

Age range
Five to nine.

Type of writing
A simple song.

What you need
Percussion instruments (optional).

What to do
Bad weather is a common experience and children can put their knowledge of such weather to positive use in a simple song structure.

Ask them to name a type of bad weather, for example snow. Then ask them to suggest two words to describe snow, for example white and freezing, thus completing line one of the song: 'White, freezing snow.'

Repeat the exercise for two further types of weather. Verse one could be written as follows:

> White, freezing snow.
> Cold, soaking rain.
> Sparkling, chilling frost.

Make sure words are not repeated. Now let the children add a chorus, completing part one of the song.

> White, freezing snow.
> Cold, soaking rain.
> Sparkling, chilling frost.
>   Bad,
>   Bad
> Weather!

Let the children try to compose verse two and verse three on their own or in small groups. Other types of bad weather they could use include thunder, hurricane, typhoon, wind, gale, ice, hail, lightning, storm, cloudburst, and so on.

Percussion or clapping could be added to create a musical effect, using for example three beats or claps at the end of lines one, two and three, a single beat or clap after each 'Bad', and a final three claps or beats after the final 'Weather'. Thus, verse two could well be written:

> Wild, howling gale. (CLAP CLAP CLAP)
> Hard, stinging hail. (CLAP CLAP CLAP)
> Loud, thumping thunder. (CLAP CLAP CLAP)
>   Bad, (CLAP)
>   Bad (CLAP)
>   Weather! (CLAP CLAP CLAP)

Follow-up
Let the class try 'Good weather' as an alternative, using words such as sunshine, breeze, heatwave, calm.

A renga for the seasons

Age range
Seven to eleven.

Type of writing
Poems based on counting syllables.

What you need
No special equipment.

What to do
Explain that a renga is a series of small, three-line poems called haiku. The haiku is a long-established poem form from the Far East. It has a structure based on counting syllables:
    Line one – five syllables
    Line two – seven syllables
    Line three – five syllables.
    Syllables (or mouth sounds) are easily understood by children. Ask them to suggest words with one syllable (me, you, it, in, out, go), then two syllables (under, into, after, breakfast, Sunday) and three syllables (yesterday, butterfly). Once this is understood the young writers can compose their haiku sequence (a renga) based on the seasons. Explain that the aim is to catch the feeling of each season in its three-line verse. Because haiku are short they can be revised and rewritten without too much fuss.

My Seasons Renga

Spring

Flowers are peeping
as chill winter melts away
and birds sing sweetly.

Summer
The sun's shining face
beams down on seaside
swimmers
as foamy waves crash.

Follow-up
● Let the children add a border to each haiku poem. Encourage them to aim for delicate and detailed drawings.
● Search poetry anthologies for published haiku poems. Type them out and mount them in a 'Haiku Book'. It will be noted that some poems were written many centuries ago by poets such as Issa and Basho!

A rhyming acrostic

Age range
Seven to eleven.

Type of writing
Acrostic poem.

What you need
No special equipment.

What to do
The acrostic is a well-known and popular form of poetry writing in schools, but it is often pooly achieved as regards content and quality. All too often I have observed children writing acrostics with little evidence of teacher input.

Explain that an acrostic has its title (for example Christmas) written vertically down the page and that the initial letters act as a starting point for each line (Figure 1). Each line in the acrostic should be an informative, short sentence.

Christmas
Carols drift across the night.
Holly gleams by candlelight.
Roaring fire, a spooky tale.
Ice and snow and wind and hail.
Santa . . . and so on . . ..

Figure 1

Children can be helped to achieve quality if a subject is chosen (for example, a season or a month) and pre-writing discussion takes place. Note-making also helps. The youngsters will then have real 'meat' upon which to base their compositions.

Rhyme is notoriously difficult for children to use. They often lose the sense of what they're writing as all their attention is on the rhyme. A short acrostic with rhyming couplets is just about within their scope. Introduce the idea of a couplet pattern of A / A / B / B / C / C / D / D. Because the acrostic is short, revision can take place easily, so ensuring correct rhymes and quality content.

Summer

Sun shines down from a blue, clear sky.

Under sunshade parasols we like to lie.

My friends

Follow-up
• An acrostic based on a season or a month can feature centrally on a calendar. Such neatly illustrated objects are welcome gifts for parents or grandparents.
• Try a 'central acrostic' without rhyme. It means that each line must be composed around the vertically written word. Animals make good subjects, as in Figure 2.

Cat

       Silently it Creeps across the back garden.
Its smooth fur is blAck and white.
   Our pet cat Terrifies sparrows and starlings.

Figure 2

A found poem

Age range
Nine to eleven.

Type of writing
Found poem.

What you need
Newspapers, magazines, scissors, large sheets of paper, adhesive.

What to do
'Found' poems occur when writers encounter printed material which they can reorganise on the page to create a message or an interesting communication.

   Allow the children to sift through old newspapers and magazines and look out for eye-catching phrases or words. Then ask them to cut out the selected items and arrange them on a sheet of paper.

Encourage the children to shuffle the cuttings until a 'communication' or 'message' becomes apparent. Some items may need to be omitted and perhaps further cuttings will have to be added. Eventually a sense of order will prevail. Finally let the children stick their 'found' poems in place on a sheet of paper.

The activity makes an enjoyable change from actual writing, yet the result is similar, and it is always surprising how many apt 'found' communications crop up.

Follow-up
Let the class cut out, arrange and mount the following items:
• newspaper and magazine titles (there will be a wide range of typefaces);
• newspaper headlines;
• different pictorial aspects of newspapers, such as photographs, sketches, cartoons, maps, crosswords, diagrams, advertisements, charts and graphs.

last night

Friday, 26th February, 1993.

SNOW IN GLASGOW   trapped   2,000

"It all seems so serious   says Gazza

At the shopping mall   jam-busters

made a   DEFIANT SCOTTISH DISPLAY

angry crowds   set a record

THE WEATHER FORECAST   remains bad

This is   THE END.

51

Inside the box

Age range
Six to eleven.

Type of writing
Poem structure.

What you need
A music (or jewellery) box, chalkboard or large sheet of paper.

What to do
Show the children a music or jewellery box. Pose the question 'What small creature could fit into this box?' The children will respond with creatures such as a ladybird, a beetle, a fly, an ant, a dragonfly, a slug, a snail, a butterfly, and a spider.

Write the following first two lines on the chalkboard or on a large sheet of paper:

Inside the box
you will find

Now ask the children to choose one creature, for example a butterfly, and select an interesting and unusual colour, for example emerald. Finally, ask the children to think what peculiar thing the emerald

butterfly might be doing inside the box. For example, it might be dancing, or jogging or spitting. The first verse can thus be developed as follows:

Inside the box
you will find
an emerald butterfly jogging,
a purple fly snoring,
a scarlet beetle mountaineering.

Encourage the children to keep the list going until six or seven lines have been completed, then end verse one thus:

Inside the box,
Inside the box.

Following this structure, the young writers can then attempt verses two and three on their own, in pairs or in groups. Stress that they should not repeat a colour or an activity inside the box.

Follow-up

● Let the class chant the poem and add percussion effects to the extent of three beats (claps or bangs) at the end of each line. A solid rhythm should build up as the chant continues.

a pink dragonfly parachuting, (CLAP CLAP CLAP)
a beige beetle boxing, (CLAP CLAP CLAP)
a silver slug saluting, (CLAP CLAP CLAP).

● Help the children make simple boxes from card. The box can be decorated with patterns, and placed alongside the children's poems.
● Instead of 'creatures' inside the box, let the children try other subjects, such as an animals box, a toys box, a fruit box or a horrors box (it could include ghost, Dracula, werewolf, vampire, monster, witch and so on).

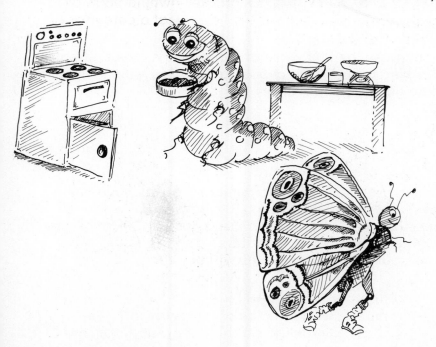

New similes

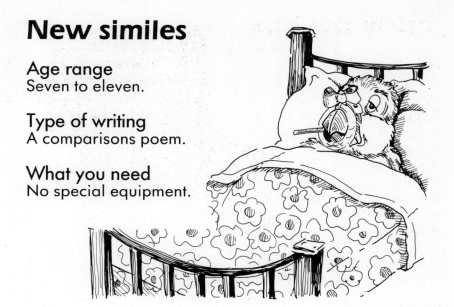

Age range
Seven to eleven.

Type of writing
A comparisons poem.

What you need
No special equipment.

What to do
The 'old' similes are such clichés that we barely notice what is said when they are uttered.

As cold as ice
As green as grass
As dead as a doornail
As sharp as a pin
As sick as a parrot

Ask the children to rewrite some old similes using new, fresh language. They should also extend the simile. For example, 'as green as grass' could be rewritten as follows:

As green as a cat's eyes glowing in the dark on a freezing December night.
As green as the holly leaves on a bush in the public park.

Encourage them to try to build a considerable sequence of 'word pictures', either as a class poem or working individually.

Alternatively, ask the children to try writing a sequence of 'new similes' based on colours. Some familiar similes that could be adapted are as follows:
- As red as blood
- As black as coal
- As brown as a berry
- As green as grass
- As white as snow
- As pink as a peach
- As blue as the sky.

as green as

as white as

as pink as a

Follow-up
Challenge the children to see how many similes they can collect over a period of a few days. Encourage them to ask teachers, parents, and grandparents for examples. Display a list of 'old similes' alongside the children's 'new simile' poems.

The horrible house

Age range
Eight to eleven.

Type of writing
Poem structure.

What you need
Copies of photocopiable pages 117 and 118.

What to do
Give the children copies of photocopiable pages 117 and 118 with floor plans showing rooms in the horrible house both upstairs and down. The children can either use the room plans to jot down their ideas for each room or write out their finished poems in the appropriate spaces, illustrating them with some of the horrible items described.

Compose the first verse of the poem as a class. Begin by asking one child to choose a room, say, the kitchen. Verse one can begin thus:

In the kitchen
   there is

Next, ask the children to think of 'horrible' things that they might find in the kitchen. Stress that you want no ghosts, bodies, blood or monsters, just simple, everyday horrible things! From the children's suggestions lines three, four and five will emerge. For example:

a rusty, broken bread knife,
   the gnawed remains of a mouldy loaf,
      and a cracked sink full of greasy crockery.

Note that the lines of the poem move to the right, giving the verse a 'slanting' shape.

Continue verse two in a similar fashion, using another room. For example:

In the bedroom
   there is
      a ripped and stained feather pillow,
        a pair of ragged, faded curtains,
          and a curled-up Siamese cat with one ear.

Let the children carry on individually or in groups with verses three, four, five and six. Indeed, there can be as many verses as there are rooms in the house. Stress that they should avoid repeating descriptive words in order to keep their writing lively.

Follow-up
• Set up a wall display of completed poems plus illustrations for the various rooms in 'The horrible house'. Let the children draw a room each, then put them together to make a complete house.
• Cut out pictures from magazines and newspaper advertisements showing beautiful kitchens, bedrooms and living rooms and display them as the very opposite of the rooms in 'The horrible house'.

Riddles

Age range
Seven to eleven.

Type of writing
Riddle poem.

What you need
No special equipment.

What to do
Riddles have been around for many centuries. They remain brain-teasing challenges for both writer and reader. The idea is to disguise the subject-matter and leave the reader to interpret the clues (Figure 1).

A riddle
A white finger,
with a sharp, yellow fingernail,
it always points to the ceiling.
Simple, yet capable of engulfing buildings.
Over hours it consumes itself.
What is it?

Figure 1
A candle

Let the children try writing their own riddles within the following set of guidelines:
• Select an object in the classroom.
• Note down five facts about the object.
• Now arrange the facts in any order.
• Write them out using interesting words and descriptions.

A young writer's riddle could then appear as shown below.

> ### My classroom riddle
>
> It has four legs yet can't walk or run.
> On its back there is a piled-up burden of books.
> It has two mouths which are always full of rulers, books, papers and pencils.
> Its brown skin is scratched and cracked with old age.
> What is it?
>
> Answer: The teacher's desk

Follow-up
Display the children's riddles in a free-standing zig-zag book, with a small drawing of the object hidden beneath a flap under each riddle. Readers can then try to identify the objects before checking by looking under the flaps.

Millions

Age range
Six to eleven.

Type of writing
A list poem.

What you need
Chalkboard or large sheet of paper.

What to do
Young children have a concept of units, tens and hundreds, but the notion of a 'million' is often confused and misunderstood. It is useful, therefore, to set in motion a discussion on 'What is a million?' and 'Where can you find a million?'

It helps if the teacher writes '1,000,000' on the chalkboard or large sheet of paper and shows how it is arrived at via 10s, 100s, and 1,000s. Can the children suggest where a 'million' can be found? Make a 'sunbeams list' of their ideas as in Figure 1.

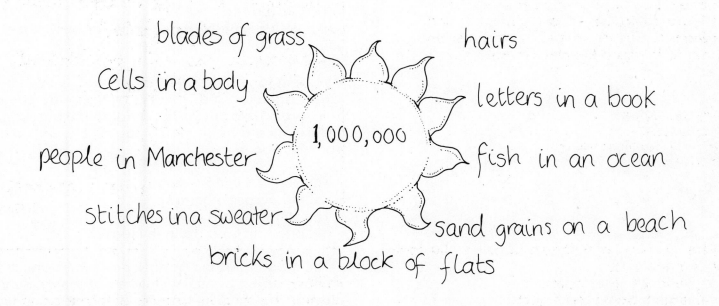

blades of grass
hairs
Cells in a body
letters in a book
1,000,000
people in Manchester
fish in an ocean
stitches in a sweater
sand grains on a beach
bricks in a block of flats

Figure 1

Using the 'sunbeams' as a reference point, encourage the children to proceed with their own writing. Ask them to shape their writing in order to give some structure. For example, a typical effort might be as follows:

> Millions
> of grains of sand on the beach at Scarborough.
> Millions
> of needles on pine trees in a dense forest.
> Millions
> of eggs laid by hens every day.
> Millions
> of grapes in a vineyard in southern France . . .

Follow-up
Cut out large numbers from sheets of black paper to read '1,000,000'. Then mount examples of the children's poems on each number. The sheets can be suspended from a beam or pinned on a wall.

What is the moon?

Age range
Eight to eleven.

Type of writing
A poem of images.

What you need
Some pictures of the moon in its various phases.

What to do
My poem for children, 'What is the . . . Sun?', has been widely anthologised. It works by using the poetic device of imagery. (However, for children the phrase 'a word picture' means more than 'image'.) Here is an extract from the poem:

> The sun is a yellow dinghy
> sailing across a calm sea.
> The sun is a gold coin
> dropped down a drain in Heaven.

The moon (plus the dark sky and the stars) offers a similar starting point for children's writing. Begin by showing the children pictures of the moon in its various phases. Ask them to tell you something true about the moon. For example, it is big and round, it is lifeless, we see it at night, and so on.

Now ask the children to tell you some lies about the moon. Ask them what does the moon look like. You will doubtless receive responses like 'it's like a banana', or 'it's like a sad face', or 'it's like a golf ball'.

Build up the initial image (word picture). Don't forget to 'work in' the dark sky. Press the children to go for the best possible words and to extend their image where they can. Here is an example set out in a four-line verse:

The moon is like
a bruised banana
lying on its own
in a black plastic fruit bowl.

Encourage the children to write other verses beginning with the same first line, 'The moon is like'.

Follow-up
● Get the children to add a mini illustration to each verse. Use colour sparingly to enhance the feeling of night.
● Mount the children's poems on round, yellow sheets of paper. Suspend some of the moon poems from the ceiling or from a rail so they appear to be floating moons.

Add a table display of reference books about the moon, space and the universe. Can the children unearth other books or pictures showing moon landings, space vehicles and astronauts?

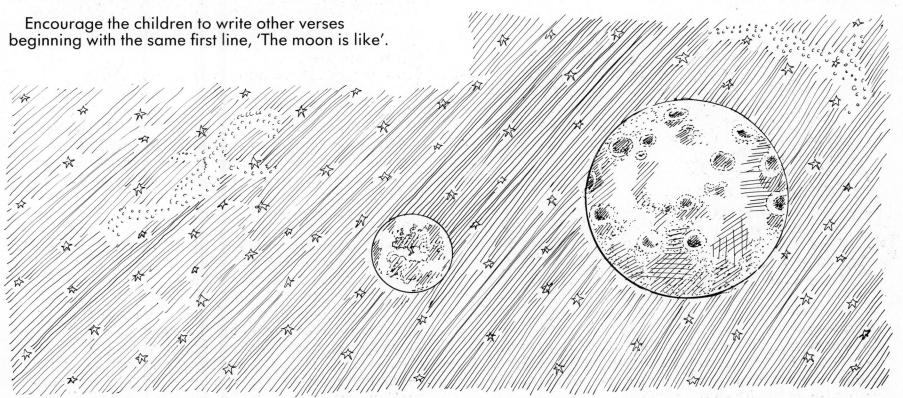

A street rap

Age range
Seven to eleven.

Type of writing
A rap chant/song.

What you need
No special equipment.

What to do
Many commercially recorded rap songs or chants are incomprehensible to the casual listener. Children can be asked to give a greater level of communication to the raps they compose in the classroom. The session is best attempted by the class as a whole or by a group.

Explain to the children that the first thing is to establish a rhythm which is simple and easily memorised. When a suitable rhythm has been chosen, tap it out on a table for example:

Tap tap de tap-tap-tap
Tap tap de tap-tap-tap

Suggest that the children use the 'street' as a subject for their rap. Explain that the idea is to describe events and activities in a way that fits the rhythm, for example:

See! Look! The growling cars.
Hey! There! The skateboard stars.
Look! Wow! That running kid.
There! Now! Big lorries skid.
Zap! Zip! The buses move.
Rap! Rip! In the groove!

Now ask the children to add a simple chorus, perhaps using a change of rhythm, such as:

Tap de-de-tap
Tap de-de-tap

Words to fit the beat could be as follows:

Here in the street
Here in the street
Here in the street
　　Hear the stamping feet.

Follow-up
● Children are amazingly quick at supplying lyrics to a variety of rhythms and on a variety of subjects. Doubtless they will want to come up with a 'School Rap', a 'TV Rap' or a 'Playground Rap'. It's really a case of creating a sympathetic writing atmosphere in which the children feel free to express themselves.
● Encourage the class or the group to learn the rap and then perform it complete with head, hand and foot actions. Complicated and highly watchable performances can develop which go down well when performed in the hall for other classes or for the whole school.

Green is . . .

Age range
Seven to eleven.

Type of writing
A colour poem.

What you need
A range of items coloured green.

What to do
Use the colour green as a starting point for a word-picture poem. Collect green items (e.g. a green pepper, an apple, a blade of grass, a leaf, moss, a pencil, a cabbage, a tin of green peas). Either the teacher can collect the objects or the children can be asked to bring such items to school.

Let the children handle and examine the green items. Then show them how each simple green item can be a starting point for word-rich writing. For example, a green leaf can be written up as:

Green is . . .
a leaf shuddering on an oak tree in a sudden rain squall in July.

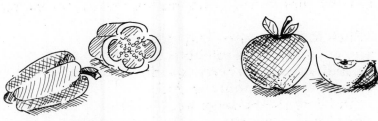

The idea is to think about the green object (where is it to be found? when?) and then extend the imaginative writing (what happens to it?).

To assist the young writers, use 'Green is . . .' as an introduction for each word-picture or short verse.

Green is . . .
a blade of grass in a vast field in Montana state. It is just one of countless billions.

Green is . . .
the stub of a colouring pencil in a tin on my table. There are teeth marks at one end.

Green is . . .
a handful of soft, spongy, damp moss. It is like a jungle-covered island in a sea of hand-flesh.

Take the writing one step further by asking the children to imagine green items other than those in the collection. They may well suggest such items as the green sea, a green planet, green eyes and green slime.

The completed poems can be written out on green paper, or in green ink on white paper, and displayed around your collection of green objects.

Follow-up
• Draw up a list of words used to denote green: emerald, sea-green, grass-green, jade and so on.
• Can the children suggest any books, films, songs or poems with 'green' in the title? Ask them to draw up a list and illustrate each title appropriately.

Epitaphs

Age range
Nine to eleven.

Type of writing
Four-line rhymed poems (humorous).

What you need
Copies of photocopiable page 119.

What to do
The idea of writing epitaphs may at first seem gloomy, or even gruesome. They can, however, be written with an accent on humour.

The epitaph is a long-established poetic form (often darkly humorous) and you will find several published in poetry anthologies. The rules for writing them are simple.
1. The epitaph has 4 lines.
2. The rhyme scheme is A A B B.
3. Line 1 begins with 'Here lies . . .' and includes the person's (or creature's) name.

An example of an epitaph is as follows:

Here lies our good friend Donald Duck,
who one sad day ran out of luck.
He got so angry in a shop
that he exploded, blew his top!

Once the epitaphs have been written, revised and polished, they can be written up in the gravestone outlines on the photocopied sheets. The children can decorate the stones with climbing ivy, moss, cracks and inscriptions (for example, RIP, dates).

Follow-up

Arrange a visit to a local church. If there is a graveyard, encourage the children to inspect the headstones and tombs. It is possible to gather a wealth of fascinating information from them – names, dates and inscriptions.

Imaginative lists

Children love making lists: videos owned, 'wanted' lists for birthday presents, party guests. 'Imaginative lists' take the process a step further by asking the children to use some originality in their thinking. For example, one of the writing tasks requires children to list an All Fools' Day spoof menu.

The aim of this chapter is to offer the children interest-catching writing tasks where the actual volume of writing is not large. There is a greater accent on ideas than in the 'Stories' chapter, but by using set structures the children can compose without endless stopping and starting. The lists should flow!

The name game

Age range
Six to eleven.

Type of writing
A list of created names.

What you need
Dictionaries.

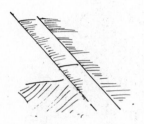

What to do
Ask the children each to write down their first and last names. Next ask them to bring down the initials to the next line and try and invent a new name beginning with those letters. Explain that this should not be a real name, but some combination of words which makes a sort of sense. Thus, my name could become Wet Monday.

Let them continue inventing new 'names' until a list lengthens down the page.

> Wes Magee
> Wet Monday
> Water Main
> Weird Martian
> Weetabix Machine
> Wants Money, and so on.

Encourage the use of dictionaries so that the children have a mass of 'initial letter' words to choose from. Explain that the lists can be shaped on the page if the children wish, for example a diagonal line, a wavy line.

As an alternative the children could be asked to take the name of a famous person and see how many variations they can invent. This can be done individually, in a group or by the class. It's fun, it's playing with language and it's being inventive.

Follow-up
Let the children select one of the invented names on their lists and illustrate it. Display the 'Name game' lists and challenge other children to match the drawing to the name.

Spells

Age range
Seven to eleven.

Type of writing
A list of ingredients.

What you need
No special equipment.

What to do
The annual celebration of Hallowe'en has taken severe knocks in recent years due to worries about the occult. Witches have been similarly dished. However, interest in spell-making remains, and with that in mind children can be set the task of creating language concoctions.

Ask the class to list all the horrible (but not too nasty) and unpleasant things they can think of in order to make a stew in a cauldron. The items can be relatively common and fairly small, for example:
- leaves;
- a conker;
- fish bone;
- coloured buttons;
- pencil;
- key ring;
- marble;
- tin of beans;
- tennis ball;
- feather;
- sandwich;
- £5 note.

Next, ask them to list each item, adding a number, a colour and some descriptive language. Explain that each item added to the stew will begin a new line.

My spell to turn a teacher into
a frog:-

1. brownish leaf from an oak tree,

2. silvery, rusty car keys from
a mortego,

3. white backbones from a codfish,

4. dried and shrivelled-up
baked beans,

5. white hairs from my
Grandad's head.

Ask the children to think of six lines to make the first verse then add a two-line chorus before commencing verse two, for example:
    Hubble bubble at the double
'Cooking pot stir up some TROUBLE!

Follow-up
• Make a 'flow diagram' illustration to accompany the spell. In the centre of the sheet draw the cauldron, then surround it with pictures of all the ingredients.
• The group or class can learn a spell and chant it along with suitable hand actions. It is even more effective if they dress up as wizards or witches!

An alphabet of alliterations

Age range
Eight to eleven.

Type of writing
An alliteration list.

What you need
Chalkboard or large sheet of paper.

What to do
Explain that alliteration occurs when a sequence of words begin with the same letter, for example, daffodils droop down in a drought.
    Challenge the children to complete an A-to-Z list of alliterations. Suggest that they begin by thinking of first names beginning with different letters of the alphabet until a full list of 26 has been drawn up. Write the names on the chalkboard or sheet of paper. The list will perhaps begin:

Amy
Billy
Catherine
Darren
Eleanor.

Amy
Billy
Catherine
Darren

Ask the children to use the list as a prompt to help them write their alliteration lines. Explain that the aim is to describe what each person does or how he behaves, for example:

Amy always argues with Aunt Agatha,
Billy bolts beefburgers and boiled bananas.
Catherine cries, calls and catches cold.
Darren destroys doors and dainty dolls.
Eleanor eats elephants endlessly.

A thinner alliterative list can be written by simply adding a single word *before* each name to 'paint' the person's character, for example:

Angry Amy
Bully Billy
Careful Catherine
Dreadful Darren
Energetic Eleanor.

Follow-up
Encourage the children to find published alliteration poems or lists in anthologies. Let them copy out such examples and collect them on a sheet (or special book), and then add the name of the poet and the title of the book.

69

The birthday tea party

Age range
Seven to eleven.

Type of writing
A guest list.

What you need
Large sheets of paper, drawing materials.

What to do
Ask the children to draw up a list of guests for a special birthday tea party. Whom do they wish to invite? To ensure that the guest list wide-ranging, include a variety of categories. For example, the children could write down the names of guests to fit the following:
- a cartoon character;
- a politician;
- a King or a Queen;
- a person from the Bible;
- an insect;
- a television actor or personality;
- an uncle or aunt;

- a character from a comic;
- one of the Seven Dwarfs (name him);
- a fairy-tale character;
- a sportsperson;
- a giant;
- your best friend;
- your favourite teacher;
- a pet (name the dog/cat/goldfish);
- your favourite toy;
- an author;
- a princess;
- a bird of prey;
- a horror (for example, werewolf).

Ask each child or group of children to draw and arrange the named guests around a picture of a round table on a large sheet of paper.

Follow-up
Prepare stand-up name cards for one set of guests and arrange them on an actual table. Get the children to add a mini drawing of each guest, some plates of food (biscuits? crisps? fruit?) in the centre of the table and a jug of orange squash. Then let the children pretend they are the named guests. Let the tea party begin!

In a matchbox

Age range
Eight to eleven.

Type of writing
A list of small objects.

What you need
An empty matchbox, a selection of tiny objects.

What to do
Show the children the empty matchbox. Ask them to guess how many small objects they think they could fit into the box. Now ask them to suggest small objects, such as a button, a marble, a tiny feather, a blade of grass, an eraser, an earring, a peanut, a piece of wax crayon, a bit of orange peel, a length of thread, a penny coin, and so on. Prompt the children by showing them a few appropriate objects.

Following this discussion, ask the children to write their lists. It can be a straight-down-the-page list with each item numbered as follows:

1. a dried pea
2. a grain of sugar
3. a tiny ball of fluff from a sweater
4. a milk bottle's gold top
5. a finger ring and so on.

Alternatively, it can be presented as a diagram with a drawing of the open matchbox at the centre of the sheet.

Do a count to find out who has managed to write the longest list.

Follow-up
Ask the children to get hold of an empty matchbox from their parents and fit inside as many small objects as they can. The children should bring their matchboxes to school when they are full. Who has squeezed in the most items? The contents of each can be set out for inspection on a sheet of paper.

Menu for 1st April

Age range
Nine to eleven.

Type of writing
A menu list.

What you need
Chalkboard or large sheet of paper, pieces of card, copies of photocopiable page 120.

What to do
Explain that the children are going to prepare a menu card for All Fools' Day. Begin by asking them to name the main meals of the day:
- Breakfast;
- Lunch (or dinner);
- Tea (or dinner);
- Supper.

   List the meals on the chalkboard or sheet of paper, then ask the children to write their trick menus. One suggestion would be to list a certain foodstuff in an odd way, for example baked butter or stewed chips. Stress that the point is to make the menu revolting but to avoid the unpleasant and to be subtle in their writing rather than lean towards the blatantly sick-making.

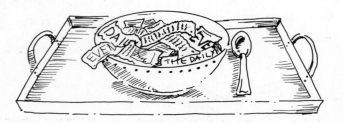

Breakfast
   Mug of cough linctus coffee
   Bowl of shredded newspaper with cold water
   Tatty toast with slime spread,
   Glass of turnip juice

Packed Lunch
   Cardboard sandwiches filled with superglue.
   A large blue tomato.

   Help the children to make fold-over menu cards, then get them to write out the list on the photocopied sheet and stick it inside. Encourage them to decorate the cover with a name for the hotel (or café, or restaurant) and add the date, the name of the head waiter or waitress and the manager. Don't forget to tell them to list prices, service charge and VAT.

Follow-up
Collect some hotel/restaurant menus and let the children examine them. Look at newspaper advertisements to see if local hotels and restaurants have listed their special offer menus.

Water steps

Age range
Seven to eleven.

Type of writing
A list of water words.

Follow-up
Cut out the 'water steps' lists and mount them on blue paper. Display the lists with pictures of water and a selection of water containers, such as a cup, a bowl, a beaker, a bottle, a kettle, a jug, a flask, an old-fashioned flagon, a hot-water bottle, a watering-can, and so on.

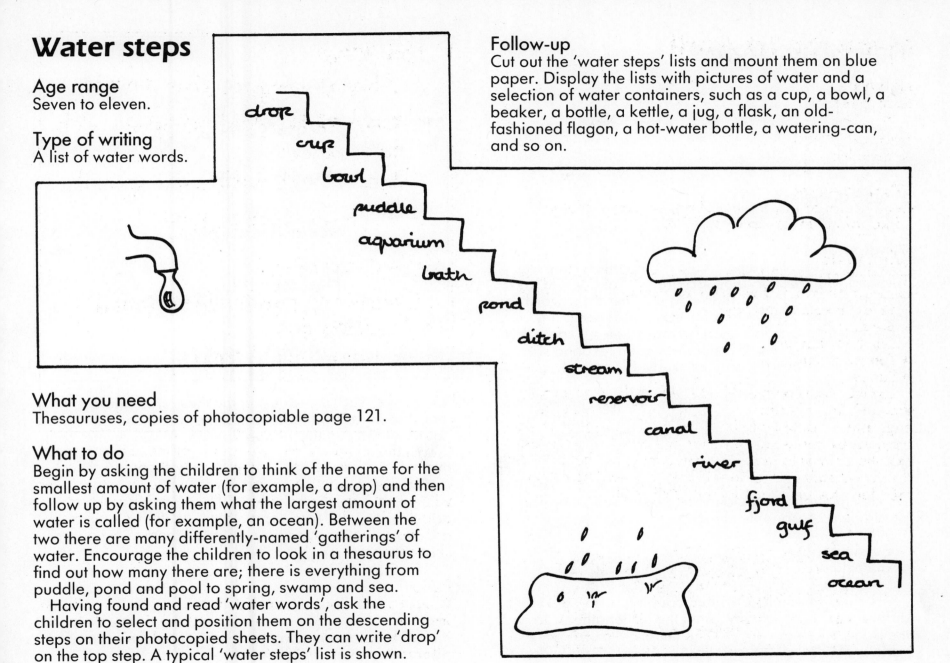

What you need
Thesauruses, copies of photocopiable page 121.

What to do
Begin by asking the children to think of the name for the smallest amount of water (for example, a drop) and then follow up by asking them what the largest amount of water is called (for example, an ocean). Between the two there are many differently-named 'gatherings' of water. Encourage the children to look in a thesaurus to find out how many there are; there is everything from puddle, pond and pool to spring, swamp and sea.

Having found and read 'water words', ask the children to select and position them on the descending steps on their photocopied sheets. They can write 'drop' on the top step. A typical 'water steps' list is shown.

Rainbow rhymes

Age range
Eight to eleven.

Type of writing
A list of colours.

What you need
Thesauruses.

What to do
Ask the children to name a colour. Doubtless they will respond with 'red' or 'blue' or 'green'. Taking 'red' as a starting point, ask the children to suggest other words that mean 'red'. Let them refer to a thesaurus if they wish. Having done this exercise many times, I know that a class or group of youngsters will soon respond with words such as scarlet, crimson, ruby, blood-red, rose, pink and even burgundy.

Once a number of colours have been suggested, ask the children to add a common word, such as 'boot' or 'shoe' or 'hair', to each colour. Tell them that they are going to use this to make a rhyming couplet. Explain that the aim is to think of a rhyming word for 'boot', for example suit, root, coot, hoot, shoot or loot, but that the word combination should make sense. 'Suit', therefore, would be a reasonable choice.

    Orange boot
    Emerald suit.

Ask them to continue writing couplets, using a different colour each time, until the list lengthens down the page. Alternatively, ask the children to use only the various shades of *one* colour. Again, ask them to draw

Black wig

Turquoise pig.

Peach hair

Vermillion pear.

Hazel frog

Golden dog.

up a list of such words using the thesaurus where necessary. This will ensure that they have enough material to keep the writing flowing. A 'red rhyme' could begin thus:

    Crimson cow
    Carnation sow.
      Rosy rat
      Ruby cat.
        Lobster mug
        Carrot slug.
          Cerise tree
          Pink flea.

This is a first-class way of learning colour words and so enriching vocabulary.

Follow-up

● Gather and display coloured pencils and felt-tipped pens. Get the children to identify and label the colours. DIY stores usually have paint colour charts. Ask for one and add it to the 'colour display'.

● Teach the children the colours of the rainbow and then let them paint arches against a background wash of light blue sky.

An A–Z

Age range
Seven to eleven.

Type of writing
A 26-word alphabetical list.

What you need
No special equipment.

What to do
Explain to the children that an A–Z is a 26-word piece of writing, with word 1 beginning with A, word 2 with B, and so on.

Let the children attempt an 'A–Z of new names for pop groups', with just two words per line. Tell them that the names should be original and that they should try to give the writing an unusual shape on the page as in Figure 1.

My A-Z of new names for pop groups

Australian Bangaroos

Catty Dogs

Exploding Fireworks

Good Headmaster

Icy Jackets

Kissing Lovers

Mexican Nutters

Old Parrots

Quick Rabbit

Figure 1

75

Follow-up
● Let each child choose one of the new pop groups and draw a detailed illustration. Make a dispay of the names and the drawings and challenge other children to match them up.
● Let the children try to write an 'A–Z of newspaper headlines', using four words per line. The last line will have just two words, beginning with Y and Z. Explain that they must create readable headlines which make sense. This kind of structure helps to discipline the writer's concentration.

My A – Z of
Newspaper headlines

Austrian Budgerigar
chases Donkey

English Farmer grows
Heffalumps
Irish Joker Kisses
Llama

Mad Nutter Orders Prunes

A sequence

Age range
Nine to eleven.

Type of writing
A sequencing list.

What you need
Chalkboard or large sheet of paper.

What to do
Explain that in this writing activity the children are going to place in order a series of activities. Below is a list of things to put on when getting dressed. Write the items on the chalkboard or on a large sheet of paper and ask the children to sequence them.

● shoes;
● skirt/trousers;
● socks;
● underwear;
● sweater;
● anorak/jacket/coat;
● blouse/shirt.

The key question the children must bear in mind is, 'What happens next?'. Once they understand the process, let the children prepare their own sequence lists for various activities. Explain that it is best to write out the actions in draft form, check to ensure that everything has been included, and then number the items in the correct running order, before writing the sequence out in its final form. Activities for such sequencing could include any of the following:
● morning assembly;
● painting a picture;
● cleaning out the hamster's cage;
● writing a poem or story;
● a PE lesson;
● the Christmas concert;
● calling the register.

The children could then be allowed to try a more imaginative approach. What, for example, would happen if a dinosaur turned up at the school? Ask the children to write a sequence of the resulting events. Imagination-stretching sequence tasks could also include any of the following:
● a fire at the swimming baths;
● a Martian spacecraft lands on the playground;
● the headteacher goes crazy.

A Z–A of things found on the school roof

Age range
Seven to eleven.

Type of writing
A list of found items.

What you need
No special equipment.

What to do
The school roof is the sunset home for lost tennis balls, footballs and sundry objects used at breaktime on the playground. Once, climbing a ladder to retrieve a woolly hat from the school roof, I was astonished to discover all manner of items ranging from shrivelled apple cores and frisbees to a multi-coloured glove and bouncy ball!

Ask the children to try to imagine the items and objects that might be brought down from the school roof by the caretaker, and to write them down in the form of a Z–A list. Ask them to try to include the following:
• items of clothing;
• playthings used at breaktime;
• foodstuffs or packaging;
• toys.

A typical Z–A could commence as follows:

Zombie rubber ugly
Yellow tennis ball
Xmas card
White woollen glove
Valentine's Day badge

As a further development, the children could be asked to add a comment or some descriptive words after each item on their lists:

Zombie rubber ugly (dull red)
Yellow tennis ball (cracked and split)
Xmas card (to Mrs Mann)
White woollen glove (covered in mud) and so on.

Follow-up
• Let the children decorate their 26-item lists by adding a few detailed drawings.
• The list can lead to classroom discussion about litter and rubbish left lying around the school and its grounds. Organise a litter collection – with appropriate protection for young hands.

The time box

Age range
Seven to eleven.

Type of writing
A list of objects.

What you need
Miscellaneous small objects relevant to contemporary life, a strong box such as a biscuit tin, plastic bags, spade.

What to do
Let the children combine to collect 20, 30 or 40 objects suitable for burial in a time box. Stress that the objects should be 'of this day and age' as the box is to be buried in the school grounds and will be dug up 50 years into the future. Suggest that it is best to choose relatively common objects, for example:
- a daily newspaper;
- a toothbrush;
- a shaped eraser;
- a badge;
- a model car;
- a wrapped chocolate bar;
- a coffee mug with slogan;
- a paperback novel;
- a soft drinks can;
- a lump of coal;
- an HB pencil;
- a tea towel;
- an advertising balloon;
- an empty crisps packet;
- a school biro.

Once the agreed number of objects has been collected, get the children to sort them and lay them out in alphabetical order. Then allocate a couple of children the task of writing out the list and making it into a scroll to read to the class. Include the list in the time box.

Ask another pair of children to compose a letter to the future, relating how the time box came into being and mentioning news and views about the present-day school and its pupils. Tell the children that the letter is also to be buried along with the time box.

Put the objects in plastic bags, then place them all in a suitably strong box. Supervise the digging of a hole in the school grounds, then with due ceremony the box can be buried and the hole filled in. If the burial point is on the school field, it is surprising just how quickly grass camouflages the spot and the buried box is forgotten. Record the event in the school's logbook and enter the date for retrieval.

Follow-up
Let the children write reports telling how, when and where the time box was buried. A sample report could be sent to the local newspaper or mentioned in a future school newsletter to parents.

If I were . . .

Age range
Seven to eleven.

Type of writing
Birthday present lists.

What you need
No special equipment.

What to do
Divide the children into groups of three or four. Give each group the name of a famous person, a character, a fantasy being or a fabulous creature. Names for the groups could be:
- the Queen
- a dragon
- the Prime Minister
- Prince Charming
- Tyrannosaurus Rex
- the Murkon of Mars
- Dennis the Menace
- the Iron Man
- Minnie Mouse
- Snow White

Each group must now draw up a list of ten ideal birthday presents for their person, character or creature. It should begin:

> If I were . . . a dragon
> I would like (for my 436th birthday)
> a dozen sackfuls of British coal,
> a red fire extinguisher,
> a Mexican princess with long, blonde hair . . .

Each group should read its list to the class. These can be printed out on the word processor and displayed alongside a January–December list of class birthdays.

Lost!

Age range
Seven to eleven.

Type of writing
A list of lost items.

What you need
Copies of photocopiable page 122.

What to do
Give each child a copy of photocopiable page 122 and explain that they must complete the lines with appropriate lost items. The list begins with easy-to-complete lines but requires more thought as it progresses.

As an alternative a 'Found!' list can be compiled, or even an alternating 'Lost and Found!' list.

Follow-up
● Ask a few children to tell the class about something they have really lost (for example, holiday luggage, favourite teddy bear). Class members can then question them at the end.
● The children can prepare 'Lost!' posters for some of the items on their lists. Include on the posters a reward and the person's name and address.

Looking, listening and talking

This chapter makes use of two senses (sight and hearing) and aspects of speech. 'Looking' tasks vary from close observation ('A stone alone') to panoramic views ('Beyond the window'). 'Listening' tasks include a walking tour around the school ('Sounds around') and responses to music.

Children are often perceived to talk too much in class (idle chatter), so this section of the chapter requires them to sharpen up their verbal abilities. They can attempt to write a telephone conversation ('Dog and bone') or create a made-up language ('The people from Pluto'). Dialogue is never easy. The difference in pace between what is said and what is written creates difficulty. Marrying the two can be rewarding and can make children more aware of everyday speech patterns.

Beyond the window

Age range
Nine to eleven.

Type of writing
Landscape description.

What you need
No special equipment.

What to do

The Victorian schoolroom had high windows in order to stop children wasting precious time by gazing at the world outside. What went on inside the classroom was paramount. More modern school buildings go to the other extreme: the walls are virtually all window! The world beyond is there for all the pupils to view.

Encourage the children to see the window frame as a picture frame. What can they see on the 'canvas'? Some classrooms will look out on field or downland, whereas others will offer a view of the playground, or a row of houses or brick walls. Whatever the outlook, encourage the children to write about what they see. It's a case of using the sense of sight.

Let them begin by making notes as in Figure 1.

I can see... a brick wall
the playground
the groundsman's shed
six trees
a flower border and
some bushes
terrace houses in the
distance
an elephant litter bin
the sky and big white
clouds.

Figure 1

Using the notes as a writing plan, the young writers can then be encouraged to proceed with their landscape/view descriptions. Explain that such writing should aim to include details such as colours, shapes, sizes, small objects and movements.

Such a piece of descriptive writing can become lengthy and sustained, so it is essential to allocate sufficient time for children to become fully engaged with the subject and to develop their responses.

The view from the window

I can see our school playground. It is a wide rectangle of tarmac with lots of loose chippings where the surface has worn away. A netball pitch is marked in faded yellow lines, and there are patches of black on the grey tarmac where this morning's shower of rain hasn't dried away. Three empty crisp bags are blowing across the playground. They have escaped from the wire litter basket.

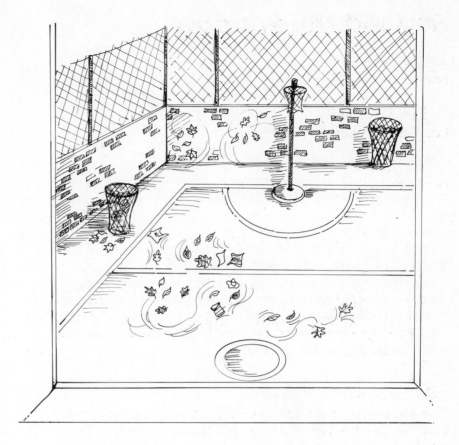

Follow-up
Let the children make three-dimensional dioramas of the view from their window by cutting out a window shape from a large sheet of paper. Next ask them to draw the view from the window on a second sheet of paper, covering it with a watercolour wash to enhance the effect. Mount the work using Z-folds of paper or matchboxes to separate the two sheets. Display the dioramas alongside the children's written descriptions.

A close look

Age range
Seven to eleven.

Type of writing
Observational description.

What you need
A collection of natural objects, magnifying glasses, drawing materials, clear adhesive film.

What to do
Let each child choose a small natural object, such as a blade of grass, a fir cone, a leaf, a dried flower, a small feather or a tiny twig. Ask them to examine the chosen object closely using a magnifying glass, and then make a pencil drawing of it, paying great attention to detail. Explain that the drawings should be at least five times (or even ten times) life size.

Once the drawing has been completed, ask the children to write a detailed description of their chosen objects, making good use of the observations made during the drawing session. Stress that the children need to concentrate on putting into words exactly what their eyes see. They can mention colours or shades of colour, shape and size, then add the sense of 'touch' to the description. Ask them to think what the object feels like then ask them to describe the textures.

Such writing is basic, straightforward and doesn't require any great imaginative leap. However, it is a valuable intellectual and vocabulary-enriching exercise, simply because the children need to change 'sight' and 'touch' into exact and appropriate words on the page.

Mount the written descriptions, and display them alongside the observational drawings. Leaves, blades of grass, and so on will need to be preserved beneath clear adhesive film if they are to survive for display purposes.

Follow-up
Set up a display of art books to show how artists through the ages have included small (and often insignificant) objects in their drawings and paintings.

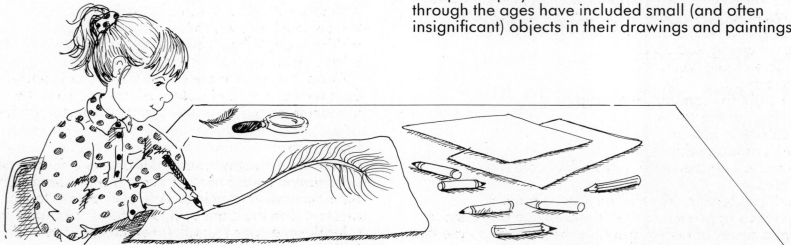

A stone alone

Age range
Eight to eleven.

Type of writing
Observational description.

What you need
A collection of pebbles, stones or fossils.

What to do
Show the children an interesting stone, pebble or fossil. Encourage them to handle it, examine it closely and discuss it. Alternatively, let each child have a stone or pebble to examine personally. Ask them to write down their observations. The writing can be completed in a paragraph or two, or it can take the form of responses to the following 'prompts':
- the size of the stone;
- its shape;
- its weight (or comparative weight);
- the 'feel' of the stone;
- its colour or colours;
- marks or indentations;
- the stone's temperature (does it feel cold?);
- its texture.

Next, encourage the children to take a more imaginative approach to their descriptions of the stone. Again, a series of posed questions helps to stimulate the writing.

- What does the stone look like (for example, the face of a jungle snake)?
- What was it on the planet Venus (for example, the egg of the Lesser Grumpy Mudpack)?
- What does it eat or drink (for example, roots of sapling beech trees)?
- For how long has it been asleep and where?
- Who found this precious stone?
- What would you swap it for?
- Where will the stone live in the future?
- How much is it worth?
- What trouble has it caused in the past?
- What sadness has it caused and when?

Gradually the simple stone, pebble or fossil will take on a personality and history of its own. Thus the inanimate becomes a weird and wonderful life form!

Follow-up
Collect and display stones, pebbles and fossils. Many information books contain useful notes about stones and often include illustrations. Add such books to the display. Can the stones be identified? (Granite? Fossil of a fern? Limestone? Chalk?) Let the children add labels to the display of stones.

Sounds around

Age range
Seven to eleven.

Type of writing
List of sounds heard during a visit.

What you need
Clipboards.

What to do
Arrange to make a tour of the school building and the grounds. Encourage the children to listen for all the multifarious sounds to be heard around the school and ensure that they have the opportunity to make notes during the tour. What sort of sounds are they likely to hear? A door slamming, voices, strip lighting 'crackling', footsteps, distant traffic, leaves rustling, wind blowing, bird song, an aeroplane, the caretaker brushing, the radiators 'ticking' and so on.

   Back in the classroom, let the children write out their lists in the form of 'free verse' poems. Explain that each note should be expanded to add extra language richness. Ask the children to write their poems in a special shape on the page.

Sounds I heard around the School

I heard
the slam of classroom 3J's wooden door, a corridor radiator bang banging as water ran, the caretaker whistling outside the window, a visitor's car reversing in the carpark, the wind rustling dry Autumn leaves, a girls voice muttering in the cloakroom...

Follow-up
● Let the children record their 'sound' poems on to cassette. It may be possible to add the actual sound effects.
● Display the children's poems and pin up a list of 'sound words', for example, whistle, groan, howl, moan, mutter, mumble, whisper, shout, scream, squeak, creak. How many words can the children add to the list?

The listeners

Age range
Eight to eleven.

Type of writing
Free verse poem.

What you need
Stop-watch, chalkboard or large sheet of paper.

What to do
Discuss with the children the nature of 'silence'. All too often silence is absent from their lives, and it's something well worth experiencing. Insist on absolute silence for 60 seconds, then ask the children what they could hear during this silence. Breathing? A shoe scraping the floor? A distant aeroplane? A raised voice far away? The wind whistling?

Write the children's responses on the chalkboard or on a large sheet of paper. The compilation could emerge as follows:

In the silence
   We could hear
the wind whistling outside the windows,
a sudden loud voice barking down the corridor,
an aeroplane droning far, far away in the sky,
the bumble bee buzz of traffic on the bypass,
children breathing in and breathing out in the room,
someone scratching his head,
a shoe scraping along the wooden floor.
   In the silence
   we could hear minute sounds.

Having participated in this writing model the children can attempt their own 'Listeners' poems. The only rule is that there should be just one observation per line.

Then ask the young writers to imagine small sounds they would *like to hear* as opposed to the actual sounds listed in the model poem. Results can be surprisingly imaginative.

The slow drip of a bathroom tap at midnight.
The swish of a butterfly's wings on a July day,
The swoosh of smoke from a garden bonfire,
The sigh of shoelaces as their knots untie

Dog and bone

Age range
Seven to eleven.

Type of writing
Telephone conversation.

What you need
No special equipment.

What to do
Children today are at ease with telephone technology, and lengthy and expensive telephone conversations are not unknown.

The generation gap within a family provides a writing opportunity. Ask the children to imagine an uncle or aunt or grandparent has 'phoned them and wants to know what they'd like for Christmas or a birthday. Stress that the point is to make the child's response as imaginatively wild and weird as possible. A sample dialogue could be as follows:

Aunt Aggie: Hello, is that Dalinda?
Dalinda: Yes.
Aunt Aggie: It's your birthday next week, isn't it?
Dalinda: Yes.
Aunt Aggie: Well, what sort of presents would you like?
Dalinda: Oh, a first-class ticket for a space shuttle trip to the dark side of the moon, half-a-dozen knickerbocker glories with added hazel-nuts, every Wednesday off school for the next six months . . .

Another telephone conversation could involve briefer exchanges in which the child receives a call, is asked questions, and must provide answers. For example, the caller might be seeking opinions about 'green' or 'environmental' issues, in which case the young writer should respond with an initial 'yes/no' answer and follow up with a reason why:

Mr Green: Hello, what's your name?
Pupil: Darren.
Mr Green: Do you approve of zoos?
Pupil: No, because . . .
Mr Green: Should we build more roads and motorways?
Pupil: Yes, because . . .
Mr Green: Should dogs be allowed to roam freely?
Pupil: No, because . . .

The people from Pluto

Age range
Eight to eleven.

Type of writing
A dialogue in an invented language.

What you need
No special equipment.

What to do
Suggest to the children that some aliens from Pluto have arrived on Earth and that it is essential for the young writers to interview the weird beings. A question and answer dialogue will result. Explain that the Plutonians should respond in an unknown language which the children must invent!

The writing could begin as follows:

Gillian Giles (pupil):	Where are you from?
Plutonian:	Beeplutobolch-er.
Gillian Giles:	What's your name?
Plutonian:	Grouppskylansker-blat.
Gillian Giles:	What's the name of your spacecraft?
Plutonian:	Kruckleduckle-yuu-firstyyy.

Other questions could cover the use of pesticides, conservation of wildlife, factory farming, dumping of waste in rivers/seas, eating meat, smoking, the ozone layer, and so on.

Follow-up
Take votes on what the children think about the various issues raised above. Members of the class can be asked to count the votes and draw up block graphs. The graphs can then be displayed for everyone to study.

The writing is, simply, good fun and the main language development aspect is in writing the questions. Encourage the children to make their question list as lengthy as possible. Questions might include the following:

• How many Plutonians are on board?
• Why have you come to Earth?
• What is the weather like on Pluto?
• What is your language called?
• How can you understand my questions?
• What do you like to eat?
• What do you think of me?

An alternative approach would be to make the Plutonian answers 'almost English'. Thus, in answer to the question, 'What are those things on your feet?', the alien might reply, 'Zzey rrr shhhhhoozze!'

Follow-up
• Let the children paint the Plutonians against a planetscape of Pluto, then make models of the spacecraft using junk materials, such as toilet roll tubes, small boxes, cartons, pipe cleaners, straws, buttons, corks and string. Mount the children's written work and display it alongside their paintings and models. Add reference books about space, especially those giving information about the solar system.
• Organise a performance where one child reads the earthling's questions while another reads the Plutonian's lines. Well-rehearsed, this can be hilarious.

Don't!

Age range
Seven to eleven.

Type of writing
Giving and receiving orders.

What you need
No special equipment.

Don't !

What to do
'Don't' is a word children quickly learn to heed, or to ignore. They consider it one of the more tedious instructions emanating from the mouths of headteachers, teachers and parents!

Ask the children to make a list of 'don'ts', such as those which might be issued by a headteacher at assembly:
● Don't fight at playtime;
● Don't kick footballs on the playground;
● Don't spit;
● Don't leave the school grounds during school hours;
● Don't run down the corridor.

Then ask the children to choose two or three of the following and list five 'don'ts' for each one:
● Prime Minister;
● mum or dad;
● car driver;
● football referee;
● cycling instructor;
● class teacher;
● bus driver;
● pet dog or cat;
● farmer.

As an alternative, ask the children to try writing a list of 'crazy don'ts'. Explain that they should ask themselves the question, 'What would be a really weird 'don't do that' instruction?' For example:

- Don't spread marmalade on the cat's fur;
- Don't go swimming in the goldfish pond;
- Don't cycle round the ceiling in the front room;
- Don't eat your breakfast on the roof.

Another type of 'don't' writing would be to ask the children to complete a list with one out-of-context word:

- Don't wear your shoes in the (bath?);
- Don't wash your face in the (dustbin?);
- Don't fight with your best................................. ;
- Don't poke out your tongue at .... ;
- Don't water the .... ;
- Don't tie up a .... ;
- Don't write on .... ;
- Don't kiss the.. ;
- Don't fall asleep in the ....

Remember, the weirder the answers, the better the effect!

94

Look! in the classroom

Age range
Seven to eleven.

Type of writing
A counting list.

What you need
No special equipment.

What to do
The classroom becomes so familiar to pupils (and to the teacher) that they often fail to 'see' what is around and about them. Refresh interest in classroom furnishings and objects by getting the children to open their eyes and prepare a counting list, for example:

In my classroom
I can see
   Sixteen grey, plastic topped tables,
   Two stainless steel sinks,
   44 paint brushes in seven plastic beakers,
   Nine paintings of 'Volcanoes' on the display board,
   One rather cross teacher,
   Eight broken sticks of chalk beneath the board,
   Six tubes of strip lighting.

Explain that the list can be as lengthy as there are classroom items to count. Encourage the children to observe and note as much as possible.

Follow-up
Ask the children to categorise the various items already listed according to materials – wood, metal, glass, plastic, paper and textiles. The list can then be rewritten under column headings as in Figure 1.

In the classroom

Wood	Metal	Glass	Plastic	Paper	Textiles

Figure 1.

Open the door

Age range
Nine to eleven.

Type of writing
Imaginative poem.

What you need
Photocopiable pages 123 and 124.

What to do
Ask the children to suggest various interesting colours for a series of doors, for example scarlet, beige, leaf-green, salmon pink, violet, orange, purple. Then ask them to imagine what lies behind each coloured door The first verse of the poem could be as follows:

> *Open the door*
> I open the *purple* door
> and I see
> a huge whale breaking the surface
> of an icy, green-tinted ocean.
> Massive icebergs slip silently by.
> The sky is snow-white. The wind is howling.

Verse two begins when another coloured door is opened.
Encourage the children to feel free to use their imaginations, and to create a complete picture in their minds before writing.

If the children find this difficult, decide on a subject area for each door beforehand. For example:
● Orange door – a castle or a palace scene;
● Pink door – a forest setting;
● Violet door – a sporting event;
● Burgundy door – a person from the distant past;
● Pea-green door – a scene far away in space;
● Crimson door – animals on an African plain.
When the poems are complete get the children to write out each verse on a separate copy of photocopiable page 123 in the space marked.

Follow-up
Give the children a copy of photocopiable page 124 for each of their verses and let them decorate them using the appropriate colours. Show them how to cut the door away on three sides and stick the sheet down over the verse sheet so that the door opens to reveal the verse beneath.

Word pictures (calligrams)

Age range
Seven to eleven.

Type of writing
Making pictures from words.

What you need
Photocopiable pages 125 and 126.

What to do
Reading certain words often creates pictures in the mind of the reader. Just by looking at certain words it is possible to create visual effects around them. For example, the word 'look' can be simply illustrated:

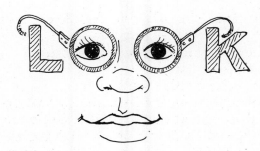

Let the children try their hands at this inventive activity. Give each child a copy of photocopiable page 125 and ask them to incorporate each word in a detailed illustration. They can use colour to enhance the end product further.

This activity develops when the children take a phrase and try to illustrate it. Photocopiable page 126 takes 'time' as its theme. Can the children provide sketches and drawings for these phrases?

Follow-up
● Make a collection of clocks, watches and other timepieces. Display books giving information about the development of timekeeping.
● Encourage the children to learn to tell the time using the 24-hour clock. It should be easy to find timetables (buses, railways, aircraft) using 24-hour timings.

Letters and messages

Writing, in the form of letters, notes and messages, continues to flourish despite enormous advances in the world of technological communications. A fun way of writing is to place children in a certain imaginary situation (for example, lost in space or on a treasure island) and then require them to explain events or outcomes. More everyday letters and messages can be composed by making use of school-based situations (for example, a note from the headteacher or classroom love letters).

It helps if the teacher introduces and displays examples, such as advertisements or joke books, in order to give the children a model upon which to base their imaginative writings. Also, the use of different colours and shapes of writing paper keeps the activity fresh and attractive.

Lost-in-space messages

Age range
Eight to eleven.

Type of writing
'Floating' message.

What you need
Pairs of compasses, scissors.

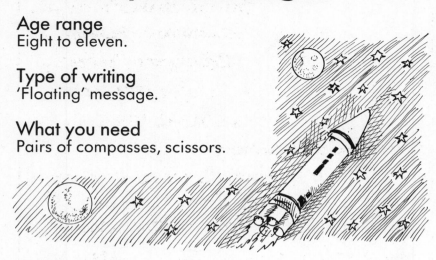

What to do
Space travel, all the rage in the 60s and 70s, has taken something of a back seat as we approach the end of the century. Yet it retains a place in popular imagination. Space adventures still supply science-fiction writing with plenty of scope.

Ask the children to imagine that they are in a disabled spacecraft somewhere in space and that they must try to get a message back to Earth. Suggest that there are problems with the transmission technology and the message becomes fragmented as it drifts across the void.

Ask the children to begin by writing the complete message. This might begin as follows:

Help! Help! This is Jupiter Mission spacecraft ZX-66. We have broken down close to the asteroid belt. We only have emergency supplies of air left and we are drifting deeper into space. All five of us have worked hard to repair the faults but . . .

Once the message has been completed, show the children how to turn it into a 'space bubble' by using compasses to draw the biggest circle possible on the written page and then cutting out the shape. In this way, parts of the message are 'lost' and the message looks like a bubble of words floating away in space (Figure 1).

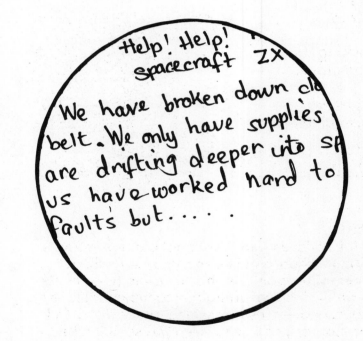

Figure 1

Follow-up

Mount the 'bubble messages' on a large sheet (or sheets) of black paper to represent the background of empty space. Randomly placed, the 'bubbles' will appear to be floating away. Add to the display books and pictures showing planets, spacecraft, asteroids, galaxies and space stations.

The caretaker's letter

Age range
Seven to eleven.

Type of writing
Letter of complaint.

What you need
No special equipment.

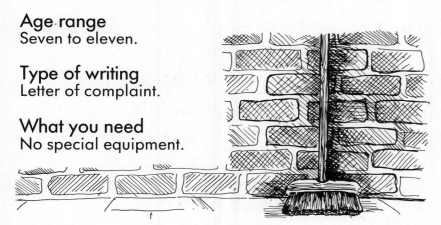

What to do

Suggest to the children that the school caretaker has a problem. She has heard noises made by something strange in her store room. As she has often done in the past, she writes a letter of complaint to the headteacher, folds it in four, and leaves it propped on his desk. Tell the children that their task is to write just such a letter.

Some pre-writing discussion will help. For example, the caretaker needs a name, the funnier the better (Mrs T.H.E. Dreggs? Mrs I.M.A. Nutter?). She is probably a well-known grumbler and is readily given to writing letters of complaint. What sort of noises has she heard?

The caretaker's room,
Nuttersall School,
Crackpot Street,
LOON TOWN
1st April 1994

Dear Headteacher,

This morning I heard a nasty noise in my store room. I was looking for my big broom when there was a .... etc.

Yours in fear and trembling,

Mrs. W.O.T.A. Scare

Figure 1

Grunts? Breathings? Sighs? Scratchings? What actually happened in the store room? Did the caretaker actually see anything? Use a selection of such questions to prompt the young writers into thinking up imaginative answers.

Ask the children to begin their letters in the standard form (Figure 1), before allowing their imaginations to run riot.

Follow-up
Invite the real school caretaker to deliver a short talk to the class to explain about his or her job. This could include descriptions of equipment, activities and of any strange happenings that have occurred. It could make a useful listening session and will doubtless generate questions.

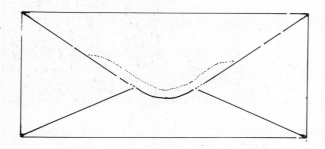

Love letters in the classroom

Age range
Seven to eleven.

Type of writing
Secret notes.

What you need
No special equipment.

What to do
Children passing secret notes is a long-standing activity – an underground communication system. Quite often teachers intercept such notes which may be expressions of love, threat or invitation.

To dear Handsome Herbert,
Will you meet me after school down by the school gate? I want to tell you about my party and ask if you'll be able to come. It's on Saturday.
from Betty Beanz

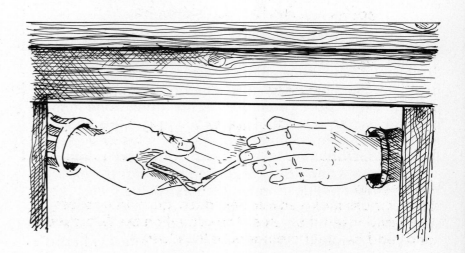

Encourage the children to invent a pair of characters and get them to exchange notes. Suggest that they think of funny or peculiar names for their characters, perhaps using alliteration (for example, Valerie Vampire, Whacker Watson, Alien Amy or Big-head Brian).

Then explain that one of the characters should write a note and send it to the other. Ask the children to keep the notes brief and to the point. Then let them compose further notes by way of reply.

> To Betty Beanz,
>
> Meet you? No Way!
>
> I don't like girls
>
> and their parties are a real
>
> pain. Don't write to me
>
> again!
>
> By order,
>
> from Herbert Hogg.

Follow-up
Let the class make envelopes, decorate and address them and insert the notes. They can then be displayed and read by other members of the class.

Treasure Island

Age range
Nine to eleven.

Type of writing
A letter giving instructions.

What you need
Drawing materials, a copy of Stevenson's *Treasure Island*, copies of photocopiable page 127.

What to do
An ancient map discovered in the old sea dog's chest helped to create one of the great narratives of all time, Robert Louis Stevenson's *Treasure Island*. Read extracts from the book and encourage the children to make their own treasure maps and to write appropriate instructions.

Give the children the outline map of an island (photocopiable page 127). Take the opportunity to introduce them to the geographical features shown such as inlets, coastal indentations, capes, bays, estuaries, cliffs and islets. Then ask them to name the rivers and waterfalls, tracks, woodland, hills and mountains, lakes, swampy regions and dwellings marked. Encourage them to add colour to the map and include a symbols key and compass points.

Next, ask the children to write their letters giving instructions how to find the buried treasure. Use the following questions to help to structure the writing and also to keep the words flowing.
• Where do you land on the island (place name, description)?
• What natural features must you locate and pass?
• What unusual things or signs should you look for?
• What dangers bar the way?
• What directions must you take? (Include points, distances, number of paces, left or right turns.)
• What tools does the explorer require (pick, spade, rope)?
• Finally, in what is the treasure buried (box, chest, bin liner)? And what *is* the treasure? (Describe it.)
    Encourage the young writers to write quite detailed and complicated instructions.

Follow-up
Singe the treasure maps and letters of instruction with a candle or in an oven. The edges will take on a browned, worn and ancient look. Now roll the maps and the letters up together and loosely tie them with coloured ribbon. Display them alongside books dealing with treasure and exploration. Some of the books can be fiction, others should contain real-life stories about searching for buried treasure.

104

The headteacher's note

Age range
Eight to eleven.

Type of writing
A request note.

What you need
No special equipment

What to do
Suggest to the class that the headteacher is cross because an unknown pupil has been playing tricks. The headteacher is determined to get to the bottom of the mystery and has pinned a note on the corridor information board. Read aloud a suitable notice, for example:

To all pupils of Sillybaggs School
Someone has been playing very stupid tricks.
Who is it?
Who left on all the taps in the washroom?
Who smeared the 'Welcome' mat with red jam?
Who drew . . .?

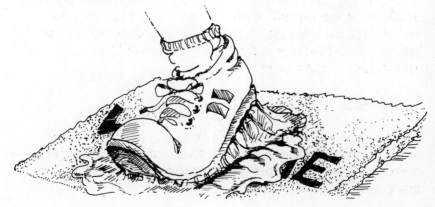

Allow the children to continue the note composing as many examples as possible (each one begins with 'Who . . .?') Then ask them to sign off the note in an appropriate manner, for example:

The culprit must report to me!
Signed: C. U. Tomorrow
        (Headteacher)

Later, suggest that the mysterious trickster has removed the headteacher's note and replaced it with one of his or her own, beginning as follows:

To all pupils of Sillybaggs School
Who tripped over his shoelace in assembly?
   The headteacher!
Who let the hamster Ham'n'Eggs escape from his cage?
   The headteacher!
Who. . ?

Again, let the children continue the list (each accusation beginning with 'Who . . ?'), inventing as many examples as possible to prove the headteacher is hopeless! Let them sign off the letter with 'The mysterious phantom strikes again!'

Follow-up
Ask the children to add a cartoon in which the headteacher of Sillybaggs School utters one of the accusations in speech bubble form. Include a child in the cartoon (the writer perhaps) responding with a speech bubble statement.

The joke notes

Age range
Seven to eleven.

Type of writing
A collection of written jokes.

What you need
Drawing materials.

What to do
Jokes, especially those loved by children, quickly bore adults, but undeniably they have their place in the lore and language of school children. Jokes do have a degree of verbal dexterity and invention.

Ask the children to tell you a joke. Many will be able to comply. For example:

Q: What did the mother ghost say to the child ghost?
A: Don't spook until you're spooken to!

Q: What do you call a man with a spade in his head?
A: Doug!

Q: What do you call a man WITHOUT a spade in his head?
A: Douglas!

Ask the children to write out their jokes and build up a collection. The jokes can be compiled in a special book or displayed on a 'Jokes Board' for all to read and groan over. Encourage the children to include illustrations or cartoons with each joke to increase the level of enjoyment.

Follow-up
Let the children work in pairs to devise a comic routine. They will need to learn a number of jokes and practise delivering them verbally with pace and panache. Suggest that one person needs to be the 'comic' while the partner is the 'straight' man.

An advertisement for pets

Age range
Nine to eleven.

Type of writing
An advertising message.

What you need
No special equipment.

What to do
The popularity of the advertising jingle is obvious and such singalongs are readily taken up by children. Test the children's imaginations by asking them to compose

an advertisement for pets. For example, goldfish swim in the nude so why not ask them to create an advertisement for goldfish swimwear?

Get them to start by finding a name for the company, for example 'Goldy Swimsuits'. Now ask the children to come up with an initial slogan or blurb, for example:

Don't let your goldfish swim in the nude!
Don't let your goldfish look very rude!
Buy her a Goldy Swimsuit!
Goldy Swimsuits are really cute!

The children can now list all the different kinds of swimsuits on offer. Encourage the use of descriptive colours to help the writing flow:
● This swimsuit has pink spots and purple patches.
● This one has black and white dots.
● Here's one covered in wavy scarlet lines.
● Try this bikini. It has yellow lightning flashes.
● This swimsuit has red sharks on a white background.

Follow-up
● Make a goldfish template so that the children can colour in outlines with the particular swimsuits on offer in the advertisement.
● Challenge the children to create an advertisement for a holiday for dogs. Instead of Disneyland, dogs are offered a trip to 'Doggydayland'. The children must explain what goes on there, what the attractions are, and tempt dogs to sign up for a flight there on the BowWow Airbus!
● Get the class to cut out advertisements from newspapers and magazines, and compile them in a book or loose-leaf file. The use of language in the advertisements will give the young writers good ideas for their own creations (for example, 'Special Offer!' and 'Hurry! Don't Delay!').

An audience for children's writing

The teacher and the child

The teacher represents the first, and sometimes the sole, audience for a child's imaginative stories and poems. The teacher is the 'reader' and can respond to the writer with appreciation as well as making positive critical remarks. The young writer will value (often privately) the teacher's genuine responses and guidance for future writing.

The group or class

At times there will be opportunities for the young writer's work to be brought to the notice of a wider audience. This can be done by the child reading his writing to the group or class or by having it displayed on a wall, a board or in a class book. If 'public' reading is to be effective, the teacher needs to give some training in speaking and voice projection. How often has one sat in the hall for a class assembly and heard barely a word as children have mumbled or gabbled their readings?

The young writer gains a sense of pride and achievement if written work is decently displayed or read aloud with confidence. Work thus communicated becomes a useful standard-setter for other writers in the class.

The school

Completed, polished and presentable writing can be communicated to the entire school (pupils, teachers, headteacher) in a number of ways:
● read out or performed at a school assembly;
● displayed in the entrance hall or on corridor display boards;
● printed in a magazine or newsletter sent to parents, school governors and education officers.

Local media

Copies of magazines can be sent out to local branch libraries (where they can be displayed), to the local newspaper (which may ask to reprint pieces, or even send a reporter and a photographer along to interview the young writers) and to local radio stations who likewise may wish to include items in a future broadcast feature.

The local community will thus see what children are writing in school, and another valuable and positive link will therefore be created.

Reproducible material and resources

The factfile, see page 15

The factfile.

1. My full name is ....

2. My age is .... years .... months ....

3. I was born on (date) ....

4. In was born in (place) ....

5. My address is ....

6. My favourite TV programme is ....
because ....

7. Three things I like to eat are ....
   1) ....
   2) ....
   3) ....

8. My favourite drink is ....

9. I would love to go on holiday to ....
because ....

10. My best friend is ....

11. I like her/him because ....

12. My pets are ....

13. My favourite form of transport is ....
because ....

14. The sport I like best is ....

15. My favourite sportsperson is ....

16. The colour I like best is ....

17. The four presents I would like for my birthday are ....
    1) ....
    2) ....
    3) ....
    4) ....

18. At school I dislike ....
because ....

19. The creature I would like to be is .... because ....

20. If I were Prime Minister I would try to ....

21. I get angry about ....

My wild week, see page 18

Date

The way to the haunted house, see page 30

A picture story-book, see page 36

Climb the mountain, see page 45

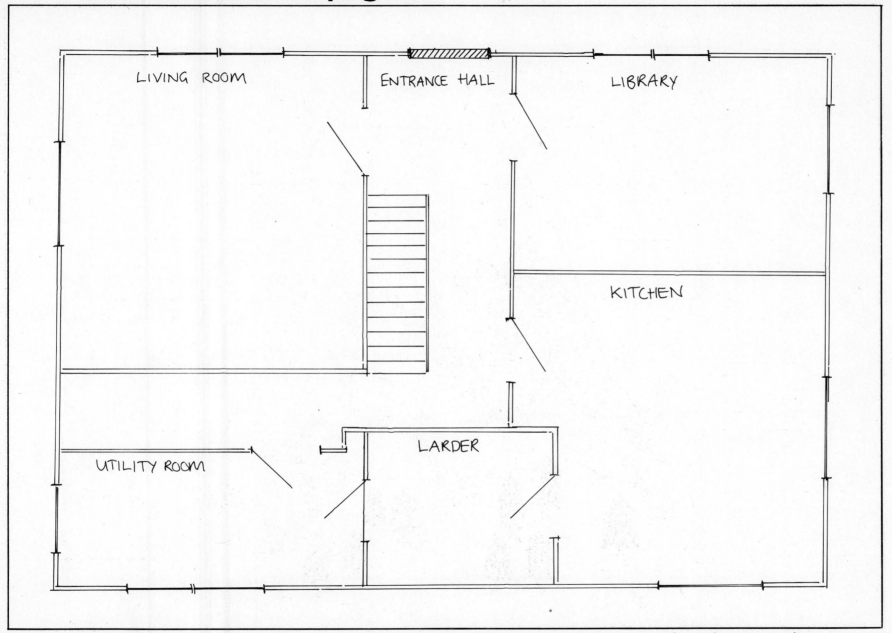

LIVING ROOM

ENTRANCE HALL

LIBRARY

KITCHEN

UTILITY ROOM

LARDER

The horrible house, see page 54

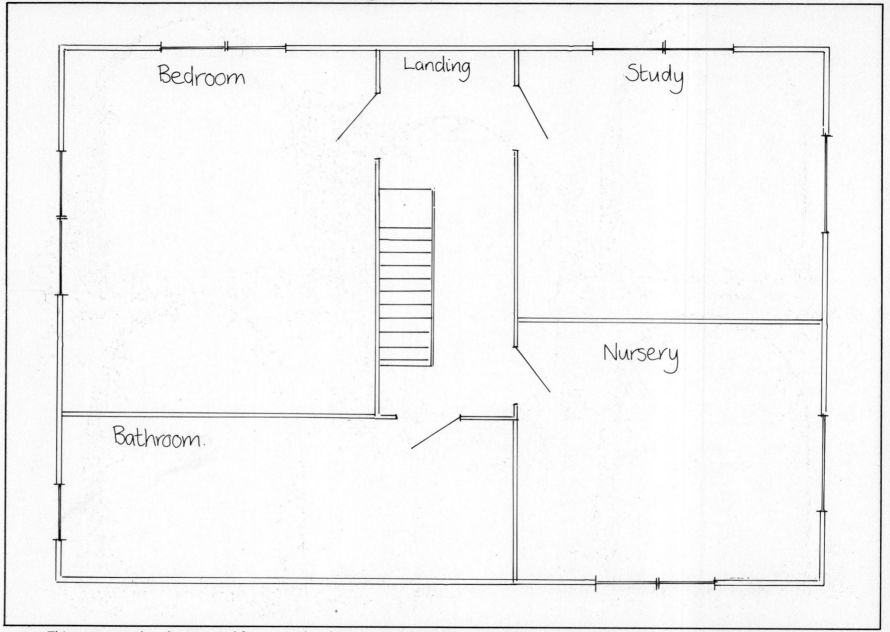

Bedroom

Landing

Study

Nursery

Bathroom.

Epitaphs, see page 62

Water steps, see page 73

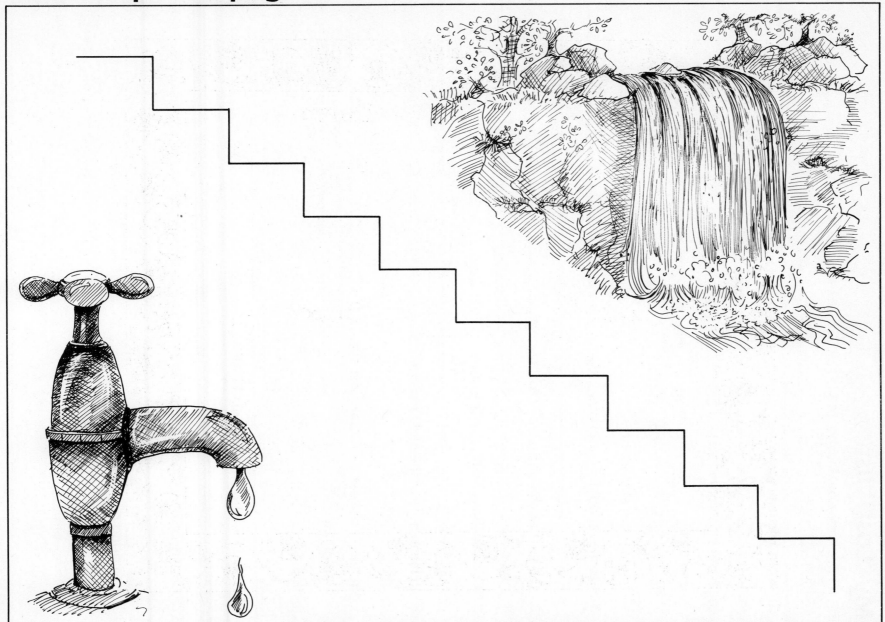

My 'Lost!' list.

1. In the bathroom I lost a ....
   and a ....

2. In the kitchen I lost a ....
   and 2 ....

3. In our classroom I lost my ....
   and a pair of ....

4. In my tree house I lost a ....
   and my secret store of ....

5. On the school field I lost a ....
   and my best ....

6. On the beach in Cornwall I lost my ....
   and an old ....

7. From my lunch box I lost 3 ....
   and 4 ....

8. In the middle of the night I lost a ....
   and ....

9. In the jet airliner to Miami I lost my ....
   and all my ...., 2 ....

10. In the attic I lost 1 ....
    and 3 ....

11. Down the playground drain I lost ....
    and ....

12. On the orbiting space station I lost my ....
    and my ....

13. Exploring a dark cave I lost ....
    and ....

14. On my birthday I lost 9 ....
    4½ .... and 21 ....

Open the door, see page 96

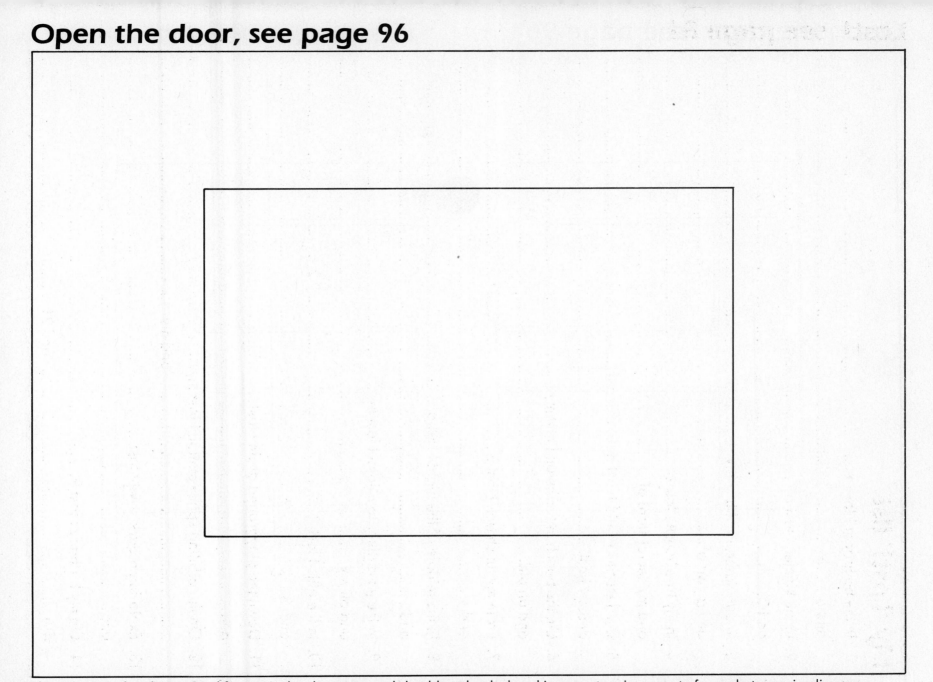

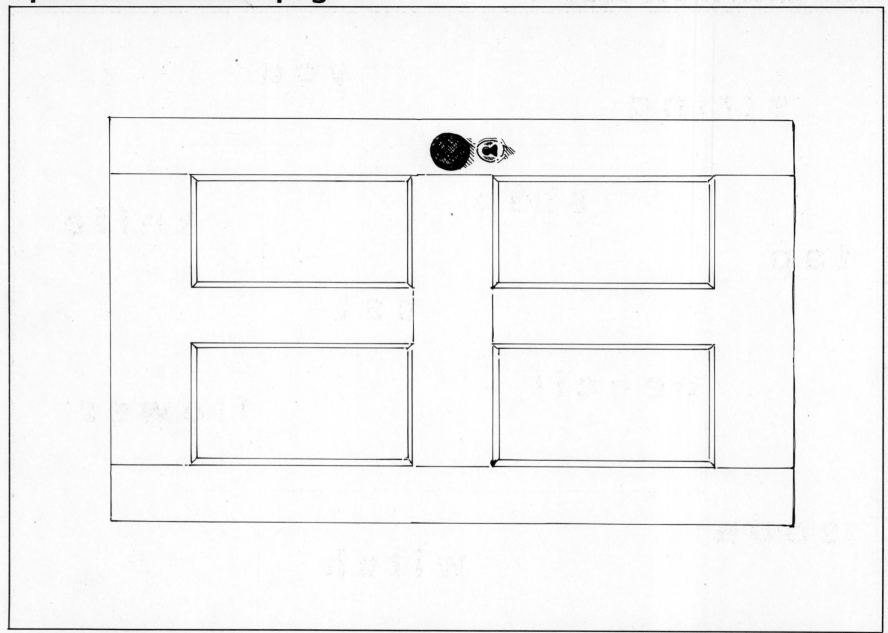

Word pictures, see page 97

you

string

stop

knife

tap

cat

pencil

flower

soon

witch

timetable   a long time

              dead on time

time without end   time's up!

              beat the clock

      time flies   the march of time

the time signal   half-time

Treasure Island, see page 103

Resources

Brownjohn, S. (1980) *Does it Have to Rhyme?* Hodder & Stoughton

Brownjohn, S. (1982) *What Rhymes with Secret?* Hodder & Stoughton

Corbett, P. and Moses, B. (1986) *Catapults and Kingfishers,* Oxford University Press

Corbett, P. and Moses, B. (1991) *My Grandmother's Motor Bike,* Oxford University Press

Cotton, J. (1989) *The Poetry File,* Macmillan

Dunn, J., Styles, M. and Warburton, N. (1987) *In Tune With Yourself,* Cambridge University Press

The Poetry Resources File (1992) The Poetry Society Education Dept

Wray, D. (1987) *Bright Ideas: Writing,* Scholastic Publications